ABOLISH ICE

ABOLISH ICE

NATASCHA ELENA UHLMANN

OR Books
New York · London

All rights information: rights@orbooks.com
Visit our website at www.orbooks.com

First printing 2019

Library of Congress Cataloging-in-Publication Data: A catalog record for this book is available from the Library of Congress.

Typeset by Lapiz Digital.

Published by OR Books for the book trade in partnership with Counterpoint Press.

paperback ISBN 978-1-949017-21-2 • ebook ISBN 978-1-949017-22-9

To my mother, and the New Sanctuary Coalition

La lucha sigue

CONTENTS

FOREWORD

This book is about abolishing Immigration and Customs Enforcement. But it is also about much more than that.

This book is about the women who clean your house. And watch your kids. And do so much of the invisible labor that makes the world we live in possible.

This book is about violence, and about cruelty. It is about fifteen-year-old girls who are propositioned by grown men, and ninety-year-old men who leave everything they've ever known behind. It is about being a stranger in your own home.

It is also about building anew.

1

HOW DID WE GET HERE?

In July 2018, the news broke of seventy people who had been summoned to appear in court for deportation proceedings. Why was this newsworthy? All of them were less than one year old.[1]

Though migration is at historically low levels, in 2018 the United States initiated more deportation proceedings against children than in any other year for which data is available.[2] Migrant children are being called to represent themselves alone in court for a decision that may well mean life or death. Often, they don't fully understand the circumstances that brought them to America— what parent tells a toddler that their life is in danger? As such, advocating for themselves in court proves to be a quixotic task. Many require assistance even getting into the chairs, their legs too short to reach the ground. One lawyer reported a three-year-old crawling onto the table midhearing—the gravity of her situation fully lost on her.[3]

1   Christina Jewett and Shefali Luthra, "From Crib to Court: At Least 70 children under 1 Summoned for Deportation Proceedings," *USA Today*, July 19, 2018.

2   David F. Brand, "Ever More Children Are Facing the Nightmare of Immigration Court on Their Own," *Nation*, July 2, 2018.

3   Christina Jewett and Shefali Luthra, "Immigrant Toddlers Ordered to Appear in Court Alone," *Texas Tribune*, June 27, 2018.

HOW DID WE GET HERE?

Contrary to the requirements of our criminal legal system, immigrants in deportation proceedings are not entitled to an appointed lawyer. They are instead given a list of legal aid attorneys to contact that might be able to help. Predictably, demand for these services far outpaces supply, and many are turned away. The stakes are high: more than 80 percent of children who represent themselves in court are deported, only 12 percent of those with legal representation are. Only one-fourth of unaccompanied children in deportation proceedings secure a lawyer.[4]

The US government has fought relentlessly against providing kids in immigration proceedings with lawyers. They claim they're not needed. In 2016, Assistant Chief Immigration Judge Jack H. Weil famously argued: "I've taught immigration law literally to 3-year-olds and 4-year-olds." He continues: "It takes a lot of time. It takes a lot of patience. They get it. It's not the most efficient, but it can be done."[5]

Key developmental milestones for three-year-olds include knowing their first name and using two to three sentences at a time.[6] Many can't speak at all.

4   "Children: Amid a Growing Court Backlog Many Still Unrepresented," TRAC Immigration, Syracuse University, September 28, 2017, https://trac.syr.edu/immigration/reports/482/.

5   Jerry Markon, "Can a 3-Year-Old Represent Herself in Immigration Court? This Judge Thinks So," *Washington Post*, March 5, 2016.

6   "Important Milestones: Your Baby by Three Years," Centers for Disease Control and Prevention, page last reviewed June 19, 2018, https://www.cdc.gov/ncbddd/actearly/milestones/milestones-3yr.html.

AMERICAN VIOLENCE

Perhaps the greatest value of history is that it reveals to us how contingent so much of the world really is. Institutions that seem unyielding and hierarchies that seem immutable reveal themselves to be the products of chance or ideology. Although ICE, the US agency that enforces our immigration laws, may seem like an immovable fixture of the American state, it is very likely that you yourself are older than the agency. Created in the aftermath of the 9/11 attacks, the formation of ICE was made possible only in a culture of fear and xenophobia and through bipartisan support for the idea that immigrants are inherently more predisposed to violence. For the vast majority of US history, we've gotten along just fine without the agency, although not—it must be said—without pervasive and gratuitous cruelty toward immigrants by other means.

To understand ICE and the environment in which it operates, we must understand what came before. We won't be able to comprehend the US immigration system—one that sees sexual violence as a tool at its disposal, that locks away children in cages, and that forces three-year-olds to represent themselves in court—without looking at the history of US meddling in global affairs. Understanding US intervention around the world helps us recognize the horrific fate that could force parents to run the risk of having their children caught up in the immigration system.

HOW DID WE GET HERE?

This chapter traces a history (one among many) of US intervention in Latin America. The full scope of US terror could fill several books, however.[7] It is my hope that you will take this chapter as a mere jumping-off point for exploring the instability the United States has fostered across the globe through military aggression and economic coercion alike. There is power in knowing our history. US complicity in the migrant crisis it now bemoans is all too conveniently swept aside. We cannot allow a nation so steeped in the violence of the migrant crisis to set the terms of the debate.

A great many academics have written important treatises on the politics of immigration. But a popular immigrant slogan perhaps says it best: *We are here because you were there.*[8]

***

America's very roots are steeped in bloodshed and dispossession. From 1776 to the present day, the United States seized over 1.5 billion acres of Native land. Whether through fraud, deception, or outright murder, the colonizers were merciless in their greed. California's first governor, Peter Burnett, famously declared: "That a war of extermination will continue to be waged between the two

---

7 For one brief survey, see Eduardo Galeano, *Open Veins of Latin America: Five Centuries of the Pillage of a Continent* (New York: Monthly Review Press, 1997).

8 H. Patricia Hynes, "We Are Here Because You Were There: Refugees at the US-Mexican Border," *AJ+*, 20 May 2019, www.juancole.com/2019/05/because-refugees-mexican.html.

races until the Indian race becomes extinct, must be expected."[9] American violence is as old as America itself.

Slavery, too, made it possible for the United States to accumulate the resources necessary to pursue an imperialist policy in the Americas and beyond. Often portrayed as an institution benefiting only a wealthy elite, slavery was in fact central to white America's prosperity. As Ta-Nehisi Coates writes, "In the seven cotton states, one-third of all white income was derived from slavery. By 1840, cotton produced by slave labor constituted 59 percent of the country's exports."[10] Despite the enormous profits extracted from enslaved labor, there has been little in the way of progress toward reparations. In 2005, JPMorgan Chase issued a rare apology for profiting from the slave trade. Admitting that they accepted slaves as collateral and owned hundreds, the corporation stated: "We apologise to the African-American community, particularly those who are descendants of slaves, and to the rest of the American public for the role that [JPMorgan Chase subsidiaries] played. The slavery era was a tragic time in US history and in our company's history." This guilt hasn't stopped them from reaping unfair profits from black borrowers—in 2017, they agreed to pay a $55 million

9   Peter Burnett, "Peter Burnett," *Governors of California - Peter Burnett. Executive Orders*," governors.library.ca.gov/addresses/s_01-Burnett2.html.

10 Ta-Nehisi Coates, "The Case for Reparations," *Atlantic*, June 2014.

settlement following allegations of charging African American borrowers higher interest rates.[11]

Through death and dispossession, the United States rose to global dominance. These ill-gotten gains at home allowed America to fund its violent interventions abroad.

THE COSTLIEST FRUIT

Guatemala, 1953. The United Fruit Company—you may know them as Chiquita Bananas—is uneasy. Guatemala's president, Jacobo Árbenz is implementing broad reforms benefiting Guatemala's poor. Among the reforms is an expanded right to vote, the right for workers to unionize, and, most worryingly from United Fruit's perspective, an agrarian reform law that would grant Guatemala's poverty-stricken farmers small plots of unused land. Agrarian reform was desperately needed; at the time the reforms were enacted, just 2 percent of the population controlled 72 percent of Guatemala's arable land.[12] While starvation and malnutrition plagued the country, less than 12 percent of arable land was being put to use. Land redistribution was not only a moral imperative but a practical

11 Michael Corkery, "JPMorgan to Pay $55 Million to Settle Mortgage Discrimination Complaint," *New York Times*, December 22, 2017.

12 Douglas W. Trefzger, "Guatemala's 1952 Agrarian Reform Law: A Critical Reassessment," International Social Science Review 77, nos. 1–2 (2002): 32–46.

necessity; the state needed to expand agricultural production to feed its many hungry mouths.[13]

Decree 900, as it was known, redistributed massive unused land holdings to Guatemala's poorest inhabitants, typically indigenous groups that had been sentenced to poverty and exclusion since the days of conquest. Though landowners were duly compensated for the expropriation of their untilled land, the mere prospect of redistribution sent Guatemala's wealthy elite into a moral panic. As thousands of poverty-stricken Guatemalans starved, the elite proclaimed that the reforms would destroy Guatemala's economy. As the United Fruit Company wiped out forests across the continent, they declared that the reforms would have grave environmental consequences.[14] Their fear-mongering failed to resonate with those systematically excluded from Guatemala's bounty.

At the time of the reform, the United Fruit Company owned nearly half of Guatemala's land. With an eye toward maximizing profits, they left vast tracts of land uncultivated—as much as 85 percent

13 Max Gordon, "A Case History of U.S. Subversion: Guatemala, 1954," *Science and Society* 35, no. 2 (1971): 129–55.

14 Richard P. Tucker, *Insatiable Appetite: The United States and the Ecological Degradation of the Tropical World* (Berkeley: University of California Press, 2000); Tiffany Harbour, "Creating a New Guatemala: The 1952 Agrarian Reform Law" (Master's thesis, Wright State University, 2008).

of the company's acreage was left idle.[15] Even so, the prospect of redistribution was inconceivable to the UFC. While Decree 900 offered compensation for land seized by the government, the land's worth was determined by the value listed on property tax statements. When the administration set out to pay $627,572 for expropriated land—per the UFC's own declared taxable value—the UFC insisted that the land was in fact worth twenty times as much.[16]

Newly implemented labor protections also threatened business as usual. Árbenz and his predecessor, Juan José Arévalo, put in motion a series of reforms to defend the country's poor and exploited. The press, emboldened by a constitutional guarantee to free speech, drew widespread scrutiny to Guatemala's inhumane working conditions; previously, such stories carried the risk of imprisonment. Workers, too, gained the right to organize under the new constitution. As historian Cindy Forster notes, "The transformation was dramatic. Before 1944, anyone who had dared to form a union would have been crushed and jailed, if not shot. After 1944, free speech in defense of equality overcame deeply ingrained habits of fear."[17]

15 Richard Immerman, *The CIA in Guatemala: The Foreign Policy of Intervention* (Austin: University of Texas Press, 1982).

16 Walter LaFeber, *Inevitable Revolutions: The United States in Central America*, 2nd ed. (New York: Norton, 1993).

17 Cindy Forster, *The Time of Freedom: Campesino Workers in Guatemala's October Revolution* (Pittsburgh: PA: University of Pittsburgh Press, 2001), 77.

In this context the UFC began an inexhaustible disinformation campaign. The UFC and Guatemala's elites spread baseless rumors of government atrocities and played up fears of communist revolt. To the press, hostility toward the UFC came to signify hostility toward the United States itself: such was the power of the Cold War ethos. The UFC also employed high-profile lobbyists on Capitol Hill, and through this access they maintained constant contact with the State Department in the years leading up to the coup. Miguel Ydígoras Fuentes, Árbenz's main opponent in the 1950 presidential election, claimed that he was approached by—and turned down—a UFC official alongside two CIA agents who offered support to overthrow his adversary. Their terms? Outlawing labor unions, establishing a strong-arm dictatorship, and implementing legislation favorable to the UFC.[18]

Operation PBSUCCESS, the CIA operation to overthrow Árbenz, was green-lit by President Eisenhower in 1953. With a budget of over $2 million, the CIA recruited mercenaries and established training camps in neighboring countries. They also provided heavy weaponry and military aircraft. Meanwhile, at a hemispheric conference of Latin American leaders, the United States forced the issue onto the agenda and employed the threat of economic and military retaliation to ensure Latin America stayed in line.

18 Immerman, *CIA in Guatemala.*

French newspaper *Le Monde* asserted: "Those who supported [the declaration] most enthusiastically were just those dictatorial governments whose power rests on a military junta and on the official representatives of the great United States companies. These governments owe their existence solely to the protection of the United States."[19]

On June 18, 1954, US-trained forces invaded Guatemala, led by Colonel Carlos Castillo Armas. Though, with only five hundred men in total, they were massively outnumbered, the mere fact of US support made defeat inevitable in the eyes of the Guatemalan army. Knowing the United States would invade with the smallest of pretexts, those within the army ranks began to call for Árbenz to resign. Árbenz stepped down and lived out his life in exile. In October of the same year, all political parties were banned from running for election. Castillo Armas ran unopposed, winning with a reported 99 percent of the vote. It is hard to lose an election when your opponents know they will be slaughtered.[20]

Castillo Armas wasted no time in eliminating perceived threats to his power. Within days of his ascent, he had over two thousand suspected radicals arrested. Acting on the advice of the CIA,

19 Ibid.

20 Kevin Pallister, *Election Administration and the Politics of Voter Access* (New York: Routledge, 2017).

Castillo Armas also created the National Committee of Defense Against Communism, a shadowy police force with unchecked powers to detain and deport. Before long, one-tenth of Guatemala's adult population appeared on a list of suspected communists.[21] Those charged had no right to an appeal.

What followed was a conflict that claimed two hundred thousand lives. To call it a civil war would imply some sort of symmetrical aggression. This was a slaughter. The brutality of state repression can hardly be overstated—as many as fifty thousand civilians were "disappeared," and 93 percent of documented human rights violations were attributed to police and military forces. Indigenous Mayas were slaughtered wholesale, burned alive, or impaled in front of their families. Military forces slashed open the wombs of pregnant women and threw their children into mass graves.[22] State terror escalated dramatically under dictator Efraín Ríos Montt. Though the conflict spanned thirty-six years, 81 percent of human rights violations— including extrajudicial executions, forced disappearances, and sexual violence—took place in a five-year span during his reign.

---

21 Stephen M. Streeter, *Managing the Counterrevolution the United States and Guatemala, 1954–1961* (Athens: University of Ohio Press, 2000).

22 Patrick J. McDonnell, "Guatemala's Civil War Devastated the Country's Indigenous Maya Communities," *Los Angeles Times*, September 3, 2018.

Under Ríos Montt, death squads patrolled poor rural areas with impunity, and soldiers forced women into sexual slavery.[23]

A UN truth commission report found that US support was essential to the Guatemalan terror campaign. Trained by US forces, with full US knowledge and consent, the Guatemalan military tortured, executed, and "disappeared" thousands. Entire Maya villages were razed, their inhabitants slaughtered, all to deny guerrillas a hiding place. In the midst of the bloodshed, President Reagan would assert that Ríos Montt was "a man of great integrity" and "totally dedicated to democracy."[24]

Years before the reforms, Árbenz famously proclaimed: "All the riches of Guatemala are not as important as the life, the freedom, the dignity, the health and the happiness of the most humble of its people. How wrong we would be if—mistaking the means for the end—we were to set financial stability and economic growth as the supreme goals of our policy, sacrificing to them the well being of our masses."[25]

We are here because you were there.

23 Nina Lakhani, "Guatemalan Soldiers to Answer Civil War Sexual Slavery Charges in Historic Trial," *Guardian*, February 1, 2016.

24 Greg Grandin, "Guatemalan Slaughter Was Part of Reagan's Hard Line," *New York Times*, May 21, 2013.

25 Piero Gleijeses, *Shattered Hope: The Guatemalan Revolution and the United States, 1944–1954* (Princeton: Princeton University Press, 1991).

REMEMBERING EL MOZOTE

El Salvador, 1981. A bloody civil war ravages the nation. Decades of repression and marked inequality have stoked widespread discontent. A coalition of socialists, communists, and poor rural peasants has joined to form the Farabundo Martí National Liberation Front (FMLN). Fearing a communist takeover, the Salvadoran government expanded a campaign of repression that employed tactics from "disappearing" protesters to bombing civilian neighborhoods where they believed guerrillas were hiding. Over the course of the conflict, the United States spent more than $4.5 billion on aid to El Salvador, training Salvadoran soldiers on state-of-the-art torture techniques. In an episode that came to define the repression, the US embassy green-lit the abduction of two students following an antigovernment protest. The students were shoved into the trunk of a car in the embassy parking lot and were never seen again.[26]

In an open letter to President Jimmy Carter just a year earlier, Archbishop Óscar Romero pleaded for the US government to stop funding the repression. Romero's sermons regularly decried violence and poverty. On March 23, 1980, he delivered a moving sermon calling on Salvadoran soldiers to ignore orders to fire on their people:

---

26 *Accountability and Human Rights: The Report of the United Nations Commission on the Truth for El Salvador* (New York: Human Rights Watch, August 1993).

HOW DID WE GET HERE?

"In the name of God, in the name of these suffering people whose cries rise to heaven more loudly each day, I implore you, I beg you, I order you in the name of God: Stop the repression."

The next day, Archbishop Romero was shot through the heart while delivering mass.

One week later, US-backed forces fired on mourners at his funeral.[27]

It was El Salvador's poorest who would pay the price of war with their blood. The army employed scorched-earth tactics to turn the tide of public opinion against the guerrillas. Through indiscriminate violence against rural civilians, they hoped to intimidate the masses into submission. In the small village of El Mozote, the Salvadoran army slaughtered more than nine hundred civilians over the course of three days.[28] Decapitated bodies were piled at the local church, and soldiers bragged of raping twelve-year-old girls.[29] The Reagan administration vehemently denied the killings, but a decade later a truth commission exhumed the remains of 143 bodies, 131 of them children.[30]

We are here because you were there.

27 James L. Connor, "A Report from Romero's Funeral: From April 26, 1980," *America Magazine*, April 26, 1980.

28 Sarah Esther Maslin, "Remembering El Mozote, the Worst Massacre in Modern Latin American History," *Nation*, December 2016.

29 Mark Danner, "The Truth of El Mozote," *Nation*, December 1993.

30 Stanley Meisler, "El Mozote Case Study," Columbia School of Journalism, http://www.columbia.edu/itc/journalism/j6075/edit/readings/mozote.html.

AMERICA, THE PEACEKEEPER

Haiti, 1915. US Marine Corps invaded Haiti, and thus began an occupation that would last nearly twenty years. Though the Marines were there ostensibly to "keep peace" in a time of political turmoil, the move was spurred not by a love for democracy but out of concern for US business interests.[31] Within weeks, US forces had seized control of Haiti's banks and the national treasury. That same year, the United States installed a president of their choosing, further contributing to political unrest. With this leverage, the United States tried to force Haiti into a new constitution that granted foreigners the right to own land. *All in the name of democracy.*

Occupation brought with it racial segregation, forced labor, and widespread sexual assault by US military personnel.[32] Before long, a series of revolts drew attention to US misdeeds, leaving Washington little choice but to withdraw. This too set Haiti on a devastating course: the United States left in power a light-skinned Haitian elite and "a legacy of despotism" in its wake.[33]

---

31 Edwidge Danticat, "The Long Legacy of Occupation in Haiti," *New Yorker*, July 28, 2015.

32 Christopher Woolf, "When America Occupied Haiti," *PRI*, August 6, 2015.

33 Robert Fatton Jr., "Killing Haitian Democracy," *Jacobin*, July 22, 2015.

HOW DID WE GET HERE?

Years later, former US Marine Corps Major General Smedley Butler would detail his great regret for his role in the occupation:

> I spent thirty-three years and four months in active military service as a member of this country's most agile military force, the Marine Corps. I served in all commissioned ranks from Second Lieutenant to Major-General. And during that period, I spent most of my time being a high class muscle-man for Big Business, for Wall Street and for the Bankers. In short, I was a racketeer, a gangster for capitalism. . . . I helped make Haiti and Cuba a decent place for the National City Bank boys to collect revenues in. I helped in the raping of half a dozen Central American republics for the benefits of Wall Street.[34]

History repeats itself. The United States has been accused of interfering in the 2010 Haitian presidential election, and then again in the elections of 2015.[35] Where it hasn't gotten its way, as with the election of Jean-Bertrand Aristide, the United States has imposed embargoes and withheld aid. The United States has steadily undermined democracy for over a century.

We are here because you were there.

---

34 Smedley Butler, "On War, by U.S. General Smedley Butler (1933)," Religious Society of Friends legacy site, http://quaker.org/legacy/co/Writings/SmedleyButler.htm.

35 Kevin Moran and Azadeh Shahshahani, "Haiti: US Interference Wins Elections," *The Hill*, October 13, 2015.

WE ARE HERE . . .

In Nicaragua, the United States funded and trained right-wing death squads linked to more than thirteen hundred terrorist attacks.[36] In Chile, they brought to power a violent dictator known for secret detention and torture sites and for the Caravan of Death.[37] In Cuba, they funded dictator Fulgencio Batista, whose secret police carried out public executions and tortured anyone suspected of holding antigovernment beliefs.

Are you seeing a pattern here?

What has America learned from these incursions? US policy remains much the same, and in a few important ways has only escalated. The United States glibly heightens conflicts across the globe, leaving others to bear the losses: an estimated two hundred thousand Mexicans have died since Mexico embarked on the US-backed war on the cartels.[38] When it comes to the United States' own role in the crisis—as the primary consumer of Mexican

---

36 Gary LaFree, Laura Dugan, and Erin Miller, *Putting Terrorism in Context: Lessons from the Global Terrorism Database* (New York: Routledge, 2014).

37 A Chilean army death squad that executed detainees.

38 Tom Phillips, "'Can't fight Evil with Evil': Life in Mexico's Most Murderous Town," *Guardian*, August 9, 2018.

drugs, to say nothing of its direct role in arming the cartels—there is nothing in the way of accountability. The United States fetishizes personal responsibility until it comes time to foot the bill.

US trade deals inflict hunger across the continent, as farmers are displaced and workers are discarded. Meanwhile, a policy of mass deportation sends hardened gang members into the very power vacuums these policies of economic extraction and instability have created. With sweeping poverty across the hemisphere and no alternate path to prosperity in sight, the streets proved to be vital recruiting ground, and gang membership exploded. MS-13, the gang that now holds much of Latin America hostage, is a US export.

The impact of US policy is not abstract: children dream of being narcos because this is the only path to advancement in their reach; families are torn apart and lineages ended; death and "disappearance" are all around. Though migration is as enduring as human history itself, it does not take place in a vacuum. It was America's violent military and economic incursions across the continent that forced families on the migrant trail. As long as the United States fails to right historical wrongs, any immigration policy it implements will be self-defeating. And as long as there are those who seek relief, we will fight.

2

BILL CLINTON BUILT THE WALL

A prayer card. Some dark-washed jeans. A tattered red bandanna. The sole possessions found on the corpse of an unidentified migrant, now known only as Case 0438. We don't know who he is, but we can piece together a few things: (1) He was desperate to find a safe haven in the United States, desperate enough to face a perilous journey that claimed thousands before him. (2) He suffered greatly. While it's likely he succumbed to the elements, his torso and limbs were not recovered. (3) US officials buried him without a second thought. His remains were found in a milk crate.[1]

The remains of 145 immigrants were exhumed at Sacred Heart Cemetery in Falfurrias, Texas, from 2013 to 2017. Nearly a third were buried in groups, tossed unceremoniously into the ground with strangers. Case 0438's skull was stained red by his bandanna.

Though Republicans do little to hide their disdain for immigrants, the record reveals a grim truth: the cruelty of US immigration policy is a bipartisan affair. Over the past few decades, the Democrats have been complicit in a swell of surveillance and criminalization that has terrorized families in its path. Policymakers may appeal to language

---

1   Manny Fernandez, "A Path to America, Marked by More Bodies," *New York Times*, May 4, 2017.

such as the *rule of law* or *waiting in line*, but we must not forget what is truly at stake in the immigration debate. Though the full extent of destruction is hard to track, academics have found a consistent pattern of migrants killed shortly after their deportation.[2] President Trump has inherited a well-oiled machinery of death.

Bill Clinton's presidency saw the rise of Operation Gatekeeper, a measure to restrict immigration at the US-Mexico border using "prevention through deterrence." In practice, this meant a militarized border that did little to deter migrants; it succeeded only in making the journey riskier. In 1994, the year of Operation Gatekeeper's inception, an estimated 180 people died while attempting to cross the border. By 2017, that number had more than doubled to 412.[3] The true number is likely far greater, given the Border Patrol's persistent attempts to obscure migrant deaths.[4] The advocacy group No More Deaths charges that tens of thousands of migrants have died at the hands of the Border Patrol in recent years.

That same year saw the signing of Clinton's notorious "tough on crime" bill, the Violent Crime Control Act and Law Enforcement

2   Sibylla Brodzinskyand Ed Pilkington, "US Government Deporting Central American Migrants to Their Deaths," *Guardian*, October 12, 2015.

3   Agence France-Presse, "US-Mexico Border Migrant Deaths Rose in 2017 Even As Crossings Fell, UN Says," *Guardian*, February 6, 2018.

4   Bob Ortega, "Border Patrol Failed to Count Hundreds of Migrant Deaths on US Soil," *CNN*, May 15, 2018.

Act. The act allocated $9 billion to build prisons and an additional $8 billion to put one hundred thousand new police officers on the ground. It also expanded the scope of the death penalty and instituted the "three strikes" policy, which mandated life imprisonment without parole for habitual offenders instead of attending to the structural conditions driving crime. It should come as no surprise that black and brown communities experienced the brunt of overpolicing. Bragging that "I can be nicked on a lot, but no one can say I'm soft on crime," Clinton stoked white racial resentment for electoral gain. In expanding the scope of criminality and targeting law enforcement resources on black and brown communities, Clinton set the stage for a drastic expansion of the deportation apparatus.

In 1996, Clinton doubled-down on the strategy of deterring migration by making migrants' lives unbearable with the passage of the Illegal Immigration Reform and Immigrant Responsibility Act. Under this act, undocumented immigrants who reside in the United States for a year or more must leave the country for a period of ten years before they can even apply for legal status. The law vastly expanded the scope of people eligible for detention and deportation. Nonviolent crimes such as drug possession or tax evasion were considered "aggravated felonies" in the context of immigration, even though they would be treated as misdemeanors under criminal law. Concerningly, IIRIRA applied retroactively, meaning that migrants could be at risk of deportation for infractions committed years prior to the law's inception. IIRIRA also restricted judicial discretion, preventing immigration judges from considering the context of an infraction. Clinton set the stage for an expansion of immigrant policing to a degree never before seen in the nation's history. In 1994, the United States had the capacity to detain 6,785 immigrants. By 2016, the number had grown to 37,000.[5]

Clinton's *Prevention through Deterrence* policy was a death sentence for migrants. Operation Gatekeeper more than doubled the number of agents along the border and invested heavily in surveillance infrastructure, forcing migrants ever deeper into the unforgiving Sonoran Desert. There, they face scorching days and frigid nights. Many have succumbed to the desert's extremes; while the number of border apprehensions has not significantly change, the number of deaths has skyrocketed. A casual observer might call that a drastic policy failure. Some say it's working just as intended.

Death by exposure is agonizingly slow. As your bodily temperature rises above 104°F, your heart rate is elevated and the brain starts to shut down. Despite overwhelming evidence of the rise in heatstroke deaths, Border Patrol agents routinely sabotage water

---

5   Melina Juárez, Bárbara Gómez-Aguiñaga, and Sonia Bettez, "Twenty Years after IIRIRA: The Rise of Immigrant Detention and Its Effects on Latinx Communities across the Nation," *Journal on Migration and Human Security* 6, no. 1 (2018): 74–96.

shipments distributed by humanitarian groups.[6] In this unforgiving terrain, strangers are condemned to death. Corpses recovered in the desert must be rehydrated before their fingerprints are identifiable. Many are too badly decomposed to be identified at all.

Prevention through deterrence presumes that migrants will stop coming if the journey is difficult enough. Experience has shown that to be untrue. But as the bodies pile up, nothing changes. Nearly 40 percent of migrant remains recovered in Arizona have never been identified.[7]

On the domestic front, too, Clinton's policies spelled disaster for vulnerable immigrant communities. Running on the promise to "end welfare as we know it," he argued that public assistance caused dependency and discouraged work for wages, reproducing tired-out stereotypes about the indigent. Thus, in 1996, he signed the Personal Responsibility and Work Opportunities Reconciliation Act (PRWORA). The bill stripped welfare provisions and replaced them with a program called Temporary Aid to Needy Families (TANF). TANF imposed strict time limits on welfare recipients and offered states the incentive to kick families off public assistance by allowing them to repurpose available funds. The results were disastrous. At the time of its implementation, 68 percent of US

6   Rory Carroll, "US Border Patrol Routinely Sabotages Water Left for Migrants, Report Says," *Guardian*, January 12, 2018.

7   Daniel Gonzalez, "Border Crossers, and The Desert That Claims Them," *USA Today*.

families with children in poverty received public assistance—that is to say, the TANF-to-poverty ratio was at 68 percent. As of 2016, the number had dropped to 23 percent.[8] Because TANF grants each state broad discretion in determining eligibility requirements, benefits are often distributed along racial lines. The majority of Black people live in the twenty-five states with lowest TANF-to-poverty ratios. In Louisiana—the second blackest state in the nation—only 4 percent of children living in poverty receive benefits.[9]

Bill Clinton poured gasoline and lit the match. He made migration to the United States not only more perilous but also more crucial. The 1992 passage of the North American Free Trade Act (NAFTA), which he engineered, wreaked havoc on the Mexican economy. The market needed to be freed, pundits exclaimed, in order to increase efficiencies and raise wages. Better still, increased exports to Mexico would yield one hundred thousand new American jobs in the first year alone.[10] But when the dust settled, one thing became abundantly clear: NAFTA was never about workers. It was about consolidating class power for elites on both sides of the border. Where workers demanded basic protections, US corporations packed up and moved

8   Ife Floyd, "TANF at 22: Still Failing to Help Struggling Families Meet Basic Needs," *Center on Budget and Policy Priorities*, August 21, 2018, https://www.cbpp.org/blog/tanf-at-22-still-failing-to-help-struggling-families-meet-basic-needs.

9   Ibid.

10 David Bacon, *The Children of NAFTA Labor Wars on the U.S.-Mexico Border* (Berkeley: University of California Press, 2005).

to cheaper labor markets. Suddenly, the mere threat of outsourcing became a powerful weapon to stifle workplace organizing. NAFTA freed US corporations from environmental regulation and instituted a race to the bottom for wages and working conditions.[11] Mexican workers fared little better than their US counterparts. Two decades into NAFTA, Mexican workers still earn dramatically less than Americans. What's more, employers left as quickly as they came, moving to still-cheaper markets in East Asia.[12]

What is freedom with a gun to your head? Mexican farmworkers were destined to fail from the start. The United States was able to flood the Mexican market with artificially cheap corn, putting Mexican farmers, many who had lived off the land for generations, out of business en masse. American agribusiness giants then rushed in to buy cheap land and set up their own operations.[13] Unemployment ran rampant, and, faced with no other option, families took to the migrant trail. Just how uneven was the playing field? US corn growers, on average, received subsidies of about $20,000 per year.[14] Mexican farmers got $100. Freedom, American style.

11 Jeff Faux, "NAFTA, Twenty Years After: A Disaster," *Huffington Post*, January 1, 2014.

12 Frank Giarratani, Geoffrey J. D. Hewings, and Philip McCann, eds., *Handbook of Industry Studies and Economic Geography* (Northampton, MA: Edward Elgar 2014).

13 David Bacon, "How US Policies Fueled Mexico's Great Migration," *The Nation*, January 4, 2012.

14 Amy Clark, "Is NAFTA Good for Mexico's Farmers?," *CBS News*, July 1, 2006.

American workers also suffered while US multinationals saw record-breaking profits. Remember those hundred thousand US jobs that were promised? Even NAFTA's staunchest defenders could document only some five hundred. The same year, over thirty thousand people applied for work training promised to those laid off during NAFTA's implementation.[15] It's estimated that in NAFTA's first six years, the United States lost a net 683,000 jobs.[16] Manufacturing jobs steadily made their way across the border, applying a downward pressure on wages across the United States. Where an auto manufacturer must pay skilled employees $20 an hour or so in the United States, just south of the border, $4 an hour will suffice.[17] Workers' rights in Mexico, too, are far more lax. Maquiladoras, US-based assembly plants just south of the border, gained international notoriety for poor working conditions. Workers are reduced to machines, expected to work at ever-higher speeds with ever-lower regard for their well-being. For women, sexual harassment and assault are just part of the job. Pesky restrictions such as safety regulations or workers' compensation need not be observed; a flat-screen TV assemblywoman became emblematic

15 Bacon, *Children of NAFTA Labor Wars*.

16 Jim Puzzanghera, "These Three U.S. Companies Moved Jobs to Mexico. Here's Why," *LA Times*, December 19, 2016.

17 Daniel Dale, "NAFTA Talks Focus on Low Wages for Mexican Autoworkers," *Star*, May 11, 2018.

of maquiladora working conditions when, her hands reduced to bloody stumps in a machinery accident, she was fired and left to fend for herself.[18]

Twenty years into NAFTA's implementation, entire families, children and adults alike, wander the fields of Mexicali Valley. Under the sweltering sun, children as young as six harvest vegetables. Their families need the money. Though child labor is illegal in Mexico, an estimated 3.2 million minors work to support their families.[19] The true numbers are likely dramatically higher—the Mexican state stands to gain little from drawing attention to the epidemic. An adult working in the fields might make 50 pesos per day (US$2.63), while a child brings in half as much.[20] As Mexico begins to import more and more of its basic necessities, food prices skyrocket—a kilo of tortillas, Mexico's staple for millennia, might cost as much as half a day's wages.

NAFTA was a race to the bottom for workers on both sides of the border. Perhaps its greatest strength was pitting workers against each other while elites on both sides prospered. Hostility toward

18 Rosa Moreno, "When I Lost My Hands Making Flatscreens I Can't Afford, Nobody Would Help Me," *Guardian*, June 11, 2015.

19 Hector Usla, "Al menos 3.2 millones de menores de edad trabajan en México: Inegi," *El Financiero*, June 13, 2018.

20 Ann Aurelia Lopez, *The Farmworkers Journey*, (Berkeley: University of California Press, 2007).

the Mexican people rose to new heights. Ethnic profiling was codified into law with California's Proposition 187, which required public agencies to report anyone they believed to be undocumented. Mexicans were somehow both at once lazy welfare leeches and greedily taking US jobs. Migrants, forced to leave their lives and loved ones behind, face widespread harassment. Meanwhile, US employers levy the threat of deportation to keep wages down and ensure no complaints about working conditions are raised. More than once, US employers have used ICE as their own enforcers, getting rid of anyone who speaks up or presents any trouble.[21] Noam Chomsky alleges that Operation Gatekeeper was a response to anticipated migratory flows from increased unemployment.[22] Violence was built into the plan.

Two decades in, NAFTA has made its mark on Mexico. The great majority toil endlessly for wealth they will never obtain. What were once vibrant farming communities today are ghost towns, as able-bodied men head north with the hope of feeding their families. Many will not survive the journey. Those who once had steady jobs now find themselves in the informal sector; an estimated

---

21 Eric Levitz, "Are Employers Using Trump's ICE Agents to Intimidate Workers?," *NY Mag*, August 4, 2017, http://nymag.com/intelligencer/2017/08/are-employers-using-trumps-ice-to-intimidate-workers.html.

22 Noam Chomsky, "How the U.S.-Mexico Border Is Cruel by Design," *Alternet*, October 28, 2013.

twenty-eight thousand small businesses were destroyed in NAFTA's first four years.[23] Poverty in Mexico's rural areas has skyrocketed. Bill Clinton's legacy is hunger.

THE DEPORTER IN CHIEF

"Yes We Can!"

President Obama closed out his presidency with the words that came to define his campaign. The phrase galvanized supporters, appearing on campaign posters and repeated at many a campaign stop. It carried a special resonance for Latino voters; a loose translation of labor activist Dolores Huerta's "Sí, se puede," it spoke to the dreams and aspirations of millions for a better world. Through this rallying cry, Obama came to signify hope. Huerta's words, after all, meant redefining what was possible: a radical promise of change. To some, he was change itself.

To others, he was the deporter in chief.

Under Obama, deportations reached record highs. More than 2.8 million immigrants were deported during his tenure—more than under any administration before him. Immigration enforcement funding reached $18 billion in fiscal year 2012, a sum that

---

23 Public Citizen, "NAFTA's Legacy for Mexico: Economic Displacement, Lower Wages for Most, Increased Migration," fact sheet, March 2018, https://www.citizen.org /sites/default/files/nafta_factsheet_mexico_legacy_march_2018_final.pdf.

dwarfed spending on the FBI, DEA, Secret Service, and ATF combined. The administration touted a focus on "Felons, not families," further conflating immigrants with a threat to the nation's security, yet you could be deported for minor offenses such as jumping a turnstile, street vending, or, in a shameless display of circular logic, entering the country itself.[24] In one particularly shocking case, a grandmother of four was detained by ICE and accused of gang involvement on the word of one officer alone.[25] This narrative of *the deserving immigrant* bases worth on proximity to whiteness, on the ability and willingness to be exploited by capital.[26]

Obama's willingness to employ the *good immigrant–bad immigrant* dichotomy set the stage for Trump's wholesale denigration of immigrants. While embracing the DREAMers, undocumented youths who arrived in the United States before the age of sixteen, Obama made major concessions to the xenophobic demands of the Right. Appealing to the innocence of undocumented youths, who "came here through no fault of their own," while ramping up enforcement against migrants with minor convictions creates

24 Max Rivlin Nader, "Yes, New Yorkers *Can* Be Deported for Jumping a Turnstile," *Village Voice*, February 27, 2017; Katherina Hernandez, "Fearing Deportation, Food Vendors Are Leaving New York City's Streets," *NPR*, January 12, 2018.

25 Aviva Stahl, "How Immigrants Get Deported for Alleged Gang Involvement," *Vice,* August 12, 2016.

26 As evidenced by pay penalties experienced by immigrants of darker skin tone adjusting for legal status. See Joni Hersch, "Colorism against Legal Immigrants to the United States," *American Behavioral Scientist* 62, no. 14 (2018).

a false dichotomy between those who deserve our solidarity and those who do not. Obama readily accepted a narrative that privileges certain immigrants and throws the rest under the bus.

Defenders argue the surge in immigration enforcement was rooted in a change in how deportations are measured. They're closer to the truth than they think. Where previous administrations favored a policy of "catch and release," the Obama administration moved toward formal deportation proceedings that further criminalized migrants. Through a process known as "expedited removal," migrants caught near the border zone could now be removed without a hearing and face marks on their permanent immigration records. In one fell swoop, migrants faced significantly harsher penalties—those with a previous deportation were a top enforcement priority for ICE—and were summarily deprived of basic screening processes. The bipartisan US Commission on International Religious Freedom found that "in 15 percent of observed cases when an arriving alien expressed a fear of return to the inspector, the alien was not referred [to a credible fear interview] by an asylum officer."[27] In the 2013 fiscal year, nearly half of all deportations were conducted without due process.[28]

---

27 Human Rights First, "Frequently Asked Questions: Asylum Seekers and the Expedited Removal Process," fact sheet, November 2015.

28 Catholic Legal Immigration Network, "Expedited Removal and Family Detention: Denying Due Process," backgrounder, https://cliniclegal.org/sites/default/files/cara /Expedited-Removal-Backgrounder.pdf.

Crimes of survival, too, were penalized under Obama's watch. Victimless transgressions, such as using a false social security number to work, were classified as "immigration fraud," allowing the administration and detractors alike to further criminalize those seeking a better life. In a shocking display of arrogance, the administration pressured the Mexican government to step up enforcement on its southern border, neatly exporting the outrage over the violation of immigrants' rights to its southern neighbor.[29]

Obama set the stage for Trump's rabid attacks on immigrant families. Though his rhetoric is uglier, Trump's hostility is nothing out of the ordinary: he is merely following a long-established pattern of mapping criminality onto poor communities of color. Meanwhile, the vast deportation machinery he has directly inherited has allowed him to terrorize immigrant communities like never before. As the prevalence and intensity of attacks on migrants scale up, will the Democrats acknowledge the blood on their hands?

HILLARY, THE PREDATOR

Hillary Clinton, too, has played a central role in the systematic persecution of immigrants. Her infamous "superpredators" remarks—in

---

29 "Mexico/Guatemala: How the US Outsources Border Security," *Vox*, https://www.vox .com/a/borders/mexico-guatemala.

defense of Bill Clinton's 1994 crime bill—set the stage for years of criminalizing Black youth.[30] John DiIulio Jr., the former aide to President George W. Bush who coined the term itself, met with President Clinton in 1995. Reflecting on his findings, he asserts:

> On the horizon . . . are tens of thousands of severely morally impoverished juvenile super-predators. They are perfectly capable of committing the most heinous acts of physical violence for the most trivial reasons (for example, a perception of slight disrespect or the accident of being in their path). They fear neither the stigma of arrest nor the pain of imprisonment. They live by the meanest code of the meanest streets, a code that reinforces rather than restrains their violent, hair-trigger mentality. In prison or out, the things that superpredators get by their criminal behavior—sex, drugs, money—are their own immediate rewards. Nothing else matters to them. So for as long as their youthful energies hold out, they will do what comes "naturally": murder, rape, rob, assault, burglarize, deal deadly drugs and get high.[31]

---

30 By the way, Senator Bernie Sanders voted yes on the bill. Senator Joe Biden co-authored it.

31 John J. DiIulio Jr., "Moral Poverty," *Chicago Tribune*, December 15, 1995.

He attributes the problem to moral poverty and a lack of religion. In a near gasp at self-awareness, he closes: "No one in academia is a bigger fan of incarceration than I am."

It was in this landscape that Clinton asserted that "super-predators" must be "brought to heel." This assertion galvanized a tough-on-crime movement that saw thirteen-year-olds tried as adults and cast aside any pretense at rehabilitation. It's no accident that her comments were made to a white audience, in one of the whitest states, just weeks before primary season. The politics of fear can be very motivating in bucolic New Hampshire.

Even where Hillary distanced herself from her statements, Bill doubled down. As protestors at a Hillary campaign stop asserted that "black youth are not super predators," he replied: "I don't know how you would describe the gang leaders who got thirteen-year-olds hopped up on crack and sent them out in the streets to murder other African-American children! Maybe you thought they were good citizens, [Hillary] didn't. You are defending the people who kill the lives you say matter."[32]

Hillary also played a central role in the passage of Bill Clinton's welfare reform. "I agreed that he should sign it and worked hard to round up votes for its passage—though he and the legislation

---

32 Ronda Lee, "Why Hillary's Super-Predator Comment Matters," *Huffington Post*, April 11, 2016.

were roundly criticized by some liberals, advocacy groups for immigrants and most people who worked with the welfare system," she boasts in her 2003 memoir. The Clintons were happy to make electoral gains off the backs of Black and Latina women characterized as "welfare queens."

Defenders assert Clinton's position softened with time, citing her outrage for Trump's practice of family separations at the border. But those who have felt the pain of border enforcement firsthand know better. Before the tides of popular opinion shifted, Clinton's position on immigration was "more conservative than President Bush."[33] Clinton has long taken a hard-line stance on immigration, declaring that even undocumented children should be deported at the first opportunity. "We have to send a clear message, just because your child gets across the border, that doesn't mean the child gets to stay," she declared in a 2014 interview with CNN.[34] She defended her remarks at a 2015 press conference, claiming that deporting undocumented children would send a "responsible message" to families. Virtually all unaccompanied minors who crossed into the United States from El Salvador, Guatemala, and

---

33 "Hillary Goes Conservative on Immigration," *Washington Times*, December 13, 2004.

34 Greg Price, "Hillary Clinton Said Children of Illegal Immigrants Should be Sent Back in 2014 CNN Interview," *Huffington Post*, August 8, 2017.

Honduras in the year prior had credible claims for humanitarian relief.[35]

It seems she's learned little since. In November 2018, Clinton authored a *Guardian* op-ed declaring that "Europe needs to get a handle on migration," attributing the rise in right-wing violence to overly generous border policies. There is no denying that right-wing populists make great use of anti-immigrant sentiment to advance their aims, but Clinton makes clear her willingness to throw immigrants under the bus for electoral gain. At the end of the day, the Democrats don't have an immigration problem. It is their failure to articulate a meaningful response to right-wing populism—in the form of a genuinely leftist platform that speaks to the economic concerns of the poor—that led to their humiliating electoral loss in the 2016 presidential election. Once again, Clinton has shown her true colors: *To stop right-wing parties, we must become right-wingers.*

---

35 Roque Planas, "Hillary Clinton Defends Call to Deport Child Migrants," *Huffington Post*, August 19, 2015.

3

ARMING ABUSERS

As the news spread of Donald Trump's electoral victory, fear and disbelief stretched across the country. One man, however, was ecstatic. Under Trump, he would finally be able to do his job uninterrupted: Thomas Homan, then director of ICE, said he's "taking the handcuffs off."[1]

Since its inception, ICE has terrorized communities and torn families apart with gusto. But Trump's ascension represents something wholly different. In the first eight months of his presidency, ICE arrests skyrocketed by 42 percent.[2] Courthouse arrests—despite their chilling effect on public safety—jumped a shocking 1,700 percent.[3] As Obama-era deportation priorities are cast aside, the agency can work more efficiently and sow terror throughout the process. ICE is emboldened like never before, and no one is safe: veterans, cancer patients, and

---

1   Josh Delk, "ICE Chief Praises Trump, Plans to Send More Agents to Sanctuary Cities," *The Hill*, July 18, 2017.

2   Franklin Foer, "How Trump Radicalized ICE," *Atlantic*, September 2018.

3   Jack Herera, "Ice Courthouse Arrests in New York Have Increased 1,700 Percent under Trump, According to a New Report," *Pacific Standard*, January 28, 2019.

grandmothers have been ordered to be deported under the new administration.[4]

The Trump administration has had its share of conspicuous villains. But some work more quietly in the shadows. Take L. Francis Cissna, head of US Citizenship and Immigration Services (USCIS). Under Trump, Cissna has overseen the establishment of a "denaturalization task force," a team of investigators setting out to strip immigrants of citizenship granted under "false pretenses."[5] Though the announcement was cloaked in the language of protecting the American people, the practice makes us all less safe: allowing an agency to make broad assessments of moral character sets a precedent no citizen would wish to be subjected to. Cissna didn't stop there: under his watch, the administration announced a new rule stating that immigrants who legally used public benefits would be denied green cards, forcing millions of poor immigrants to turn down desperately needed assistance.[6]

Under Trump, the nature of enforcement changed radically. Where his more ambitious plans—such as the Muslim ban or eliminating

---

4   Theresa Waldrop, "US Army Veteran Who Served Two Tours in Afghanistan Has Been Deported to Mexico," *CNN*, March 26, 2018; Bill Kirkos, "Woman Dying of Cancer Seeks Deportation Stay," *CNN*, August 10, 2018; Elizabeth Elizalde and Larry McShane, "Feds Secretly Deport Brooklyn Grandmom to Mexico after 33 Years, Stunning Family Members," *NY Daily News*, September 19, 2018.

5   Ted Hesson, "The Man behind Trump's 'Invisible Wall,'" *Politico*, September 20, 2018.

6   Michael D. Hear and Emily Baumbaertner, "Trump Administration Aims to Sharply Restrict New Green Cards for Those on Public Aid," *New York Times*, September 22, 2018.

domestic abuse as a protected category for asylum—were promptly challenged, a few more insidious changes took hold. The administration came to favor a policy known as "attrition through enforcement," whereby conditions for immigrants become so inhumane that some choose to self-deport. Kris Kobach, former Kansas secretary of state, laid it out: "Illegal aliens are rational decision makers. If the risks of detention or involuntary removal go up, and the probability of being able to obtain unauthorized employment goes down, then at some point, the only rational decision is to return home." Perversely, then, even Trump's failed stunts still yield the desired effect: fostering a climate of fear.[7]

As part of that strategy, the administration has employed an unyielding ideological campaign against migrants seeking safety. In May 2018, the White House published an article titled: "What You Need to Know about the Violent Animals of MS-13." In a memo of fewer than five hundred words, the administration used the word "animals" ten times.[8] The intent is clear: to conflate Salvadoran asylum seekers with the very gangs that terrorize them into fleeing. Of course, no mention is made of US culpability in creating and fueling the gang crisis in Central America. By the time activists and journalists point this out, the damage has been done: *all* immigrants are now suspect.

---

7   Foer, "How Trump Radicalized ICE."

8   "What You Need to Know about the Violent Animals of MS-13," White House, May 21, 2018.

ARMING ABUSERS

The Democratic Party, for its part, has offered little in the way of resistance. Time and time again they have capitulated to Republican demands, even where victory lay within reach. The problem is simple: ultimately the Democrats don't differ as much from Republicans as we might like to think. The Democrats have accepted wholesale the Republican framing of an immigration "crisis" and readily accept the need for increased enforcement in the name of safety. Sure, they may decry the GOP's more barbaric impulses—such as SB1070[9] and Trump's posturing for a wall—but their outrage means little when they have presided over some of the most extreme border militarization in our nation's history.

There are, of course, exceptions: Alexandria Ocasio-Cortez won a historic election, campaigning on the promise to abolish ICE. In a landslide victory, she unseated an opponent who had represented the district since 1999. Her success has inspired a wave of challengers targeting contested seats from the left, prompting comfortable Democratic incumbents in New York State to engage with more progressive policy demands. Ilhan Omar and Rashida Tlaib also made history in 2019 as the first two Muslim women

9   Reviled by critics for its "show me your papers" provision, the law requires Arizona law enforcement officers to determine a person's immigration status if they have reasonable suspicion that they are undocumented. The law has been challenged in the courts since its inception, given its reliance on racial profiling.

elected to Congress.[10] Their campaigns, too, centered the demand to abolish ICE. These victories demonstrate a desire for a true progressive agenda.

The Trump administration has elevated the worst impulses of our immigration system. But there is danger in seeing Trump's cruelty as a wholly new phenomenon. A system that assumes nefarious intent on the part of immigrants significantly predates Trump and his ilk.

DON'T WAIT UNTIL WE'RE MARTYRS

What is the outcome of this bipartisan hostility? A blood-stained journey. Even as fewer take off on the migrant trail, border deaths are up.[11]

I spoke with Justine, a volunteer with the immigrant advocacy group No More Deaths. The group distributes water throughout the arid Sonoran Desert to prevent migrant deaths along the border. Earlier this year, they drew attention to the Border Patrol's systematic destruction of water drops left for migrants. Within hours, footage of Border Patrol agents emptying water jugs had drawn over two hundred thousand views. That same day, Border

10 Michelle Boorstein, Marisa Iati, and Julie Zauzmer, "The Nation's First Two Muslim Congresswomen Are Sworn in, Surrounded by the Women They Inspired," *Washington Post*, January 3, 2019.

11 Kendal Blust, "Deaths per 10,000 Border Crossers Are Up 5 Times from a Decade Ago," *Arizona Daily Star*, May 21, 2016.

Patrol agents arrested Scott Warren, a college instructor and No More Deaths volunteer, on charges of harboring migrants. He faces two decades in prison if convicted.

"For folks who have never traveled through the Sonoran Desert, it is crucial to understand that it is physically impossible for a human being to carry enough water to hike on foot through the corridors most migrants pass through from the border into the United States," notes Justine.

"In the summer," Justine explained, "temperatures in southern Arizona and northern Mexico easily reach 115 to 120 degrees Fahrenheit, and in the winter, temperatures can drop below freezing. This is where Clinton's policy of Prevention through Deterrence comes into play: in the mid-1990s, urban areas were walled off, checkpoints were added strategically along major roads and routes, and there was a sharp increase in agents patrolling the border. Where deaths along the border were previously low, numbers quickly multiplied. The goal of Prevention through Deterrence was to push those crossing without papers into the most dangerous parts of the desert so as to avoid detection. The US government knew people would die, and argued that this would deter other crossers. But with nearly eighty-five hundred remains recovered since the mid-1990s in the Sonoran Desert (and that is just remains found—we have to estimate the numbers are much higher, given the rapid rate of decomposition in such extreme conditions), Prevention through Deterrence has only served to make the desert a weapon of Border Patrol. So long as the root causes of forced migration remain unaddressed, people will continue to risk their lives crossing in search of safety. To die in the desert, as so many have, is a painful, slow, lonely, and blistering death, that no one should suffer through."

Prevention through Deterrence has forced migrants ever deeper into desolate terrain. As No More Deaths highlights in their *Disappeared* report, the Border Patrol's very indicators of success for the program are violent to their core. They include "fee increases by smugglers," "possible increases in complaints," and "more violence at attempted entries." Border Patrol cannot feign ignorance of the death and dispossession they have wrought. It's built into the plan.

The Border Patrol itself claims that some six thousand migrants have died crossing into the United States since the 1990s. However, evidence suggests the agency drastically undercounts the number of border deaths.[12] Even if they were operating in good faith—that's giving a lot of credit to an agency whose benchmarks for success involve hastening preventable deaths—tracking death in the desert is a tall order. In 2014, a group of anthropologists set out to investigate bodily decomposition patterns in the Sonoran Desert. They dressed pig carcasses in the sort of clothes worn by migrants, alongside personal effects like wallets and identification,

---

12 La Coalición de Derechos Humanos and No More Deaths, *Disappeared: How the US Border Enforcement Agencies Are Fueling a Missing Persons Crisis*, http://www.the disappearedreport.org.

and left them in the desert. Within five days, animal scavengers had approached the corpse. Two days later, a domestic dog was found chewing on the corpse's ruptured intestines. Within weeks, most of the bones had been scattered across the desert.[13] Within two months, the academics conclude, "skeletal regions most useful for forensic identification are unlikely to be well preserved." After this point, DNA analysis is necessary to identify the remains. *So neatly is the Border Patrol's complicity swept through the sands.*

Sandra,[14] an undocumented migrant now seeking asylum on the East Coast, knows the pain of the deterrence policy firsthand. "[Border Patrol agents] scattered us, had us running in different directions. We were terrified. It was the scariest thing I've ever done, but I needed to." She reflects a moment. "My nephew, he crossed two months ago. We still haven't heard from him."

As the border becomes increasingly militarized, migrants are pushed deeper into arid and inaccessible terrain. There, they face deadly weather extremes and dehydration—and that's if they're lucky. Extortion by narcos is increasingly common.[15] Stories of rape

---

13 Jess Beck, Ian Ostericher, Gregory Sollish, and Jason De Leon, "Animal Scavenging and Scattering and the Implications for Documenting the Deaths of Undocumented Border Crossers in the Sonoran Desert," *Journal of Forensic Sciences* 60, supp. 1 (2014): S11–20.

14 Name has been changed for privacy.

15 Jason Beaubien, "Brutal Cartels Make Crossing U.S. Border Even Riskier," *NPR*, July 8, 2011.

along the migrant trail are so common that some bring birth control on the journey.[16] The United States has effectively created a human trafficking industry.

THE BODIES THEY DON'T CLAIM

The border enforces a hierarchy premised on the accident of birth. Your place of birth determines the world you live in: what economic opportunities are available to you, the quality of the schools your children will attend, whether anyone will grieve at the sight of your corpse—or if it will be tossed in a milk crate with nearby debris. The forces that send families on the migrant trail are dense and intertwined, but one thing is clear: US policy spurs migration around the globe.

One would think the disastrous legacy of NAFTA would have served as a warning. But in 2005 the free trade agreement was expanded to include Guatemala, El Salvador, Honduras, Costa Rica, and Nicaragua in the form of CAFTA, the Central American Free Trade Agreement. The results, predictably, are equally as dire as those of its predecessor. CAFTA granted multinationals vast monopoly protections, leaving Central America's poor to foot the bill. In Guatemala, CAFTA rescinded access to generic heart attack medication that was

16 Jude Joffe-Block, "Women Crossing the U.S. Border Face Sexual Assault with Little Protection," *PBS Newshour*, March 13, 2014.

previously widely available, granting exclusive market rights to its patented variant.[17] Meanwhile, other producers of generic drugs have been denied entry to the Guatemalan market altogether, with "drugs [used] to treat major causes of mortality and morbidity" restricted to their brand-name counterparts.[18] The advent of CAFTA has also seen "systematic and systemic gaps" in the enforcement of labor laws and has generated violence against union members.[19]

Where military intervention has failed, extractive economic policy has finished the job. Latin America has been systematically excluded from all but the lowest rungs of the global economy.

***

Love letters. Cigarettes. A frayed dollar bill. At the Office of the Medical Examiner in Tucson, Arizona, forensic anthropologist Bruce Anderson works to identify migrant remains found in the desert. Given how quickly bodies decompose in the heat, he works with limited information, from bone fragments to personal items found near remains.

The desert that claims these migrants is as unforgiving in life as it is in death. Forensic evidence was not made for this world.

---

17 Ellen R. Shaffer and Joseph E. Brenner, "A Trade Agreement's Impact on Access to Generic Drugs," *Health Affairs*, October 2009.

18 Ibid.

19 Eric Gottwald and Jeffrey Vogt, "Wrong Turn for Workers' Rights: The US-Guatemala CAFTA Labor Arbitration Ruling—And What to Do About It," International Labor Rights Forum, April 12, 2018.

Fingerprints are so dried out they must be rehydrated before yielding information; bodies so ravaged they're often identifiable only by dental records. Coyotes and other scavengers can spread bone fragments miles across the desert. They say death doesn't discriminate. But the Sonoran Desert tells a different tale. Imagine for a moment that you are the medical examiner trying to identify the latest body. The face, if it remains, is a wrinkled, dehydrated visage. There is no wallet. The fingers have been eaten by scavengers. You are left with two options: dental records or DNA. Not surprisingly, a great many of these deceased migrants never saw the inside of a dentist's office, and many of their families who could come forward and provide DNA for identification do not, for fear of deportation. Structural vulnerability is nowhere more visible than here, where the sort of journey migrants undergo maps neatly along racial and class lines. Whether you walk or drive through the brunt of the desert, and whether you're pushed out of your home in the first place, is directly informed by social positioning. While Latin America as a whole has been systematically exploited, the people of Latin America also face discrimination based on color and class. Status matters, even after death. "The stresses of poverty are written in their skin, in their bones, and in their teeth," Anderson notes.

Anderson's caseload has grown dramatically with the advent of deterrence policies. From 1990 to 1999, an average of 12 migrants died per year in southern Arizona. Between 2000 to 2017, that number rose to 157 per year.[20] "Every other day, we're looking at a body or a sun-bleached bone." Anderson asserts.

Death comes slowly in the arid terrain.

Survivors talk about people "going crazy"; in the final stages of hyperthermia, it's not uncommon for people to tear off their clothes in desperation. The scrapes and gashes found on many of the cadavers testify to this. The atrocities continue. "Every year we get two or three hangings. We assume they're suicides; they're kneeling with their belt or shoelaces around their neck. We think, or hope, that they're not witnessed, that they were in isolation and nobody could help them . . . Can you imagine being so uncomfortable, so hot or thirsty that hanging yourself is better than that?" Anderson's eyes trail off, lost in thought.

Finding decomposed bodies in any other part of the United States would cause widespread panic. But to the US Border Patrol, life is cheap. Deterrence strategies keep the problem neatly out of sight and allow US policymakers to push the costs of migration—the burden of death—onto the poor and dispossessed. Day after day, outrage after outrage, little changes in the desert.

At the medical examiner's office, the bodies continue to pile up. Dr. Anderson and his team keep meticulous records of any scraps or personal effects that can help identify the deceased. Their last earthly possessions fit neatly in ziplock plastic bags.

20 Colibrí Center, "Our History," www.colibricenter.org/history.

It's quiet in the desert. Stifling, as if death itself cried out for respite.

By pushing traffic into the most remote parts of the desert, America has sentenced thousands to death via bipartisan consensus. But the cruelty of US immigration policy does not end here. Those who survive the journey still face the constant threat of immigration enforcement and death by deportation.

RONALD'S DOWNFALL

Ronald Acevedo predicted his own death.

The signs were clear to anyone who was looking: phone calls, text messages, even handwritten letters stating the gang's intention to kill him.

Ronald left home. He had a strong case, he thought; El Salvador was the murder capital of the world, and several friends had already died at the hands of the gang. So, in April 2017, he crossed into Arizona and promptly turned himself in to immigration officials.

He was wrong. He spent eight months in detention before withdrawing his asylum claim. Immigration officers had told him he had no chance of winning it.[21]

---

21 Kevin Sieff, "When Death Awaits Deported Asylum Seekers," *Washington Post*, December 26, 2018.

Ronald was deported to El Salvador on November 29, 2017. Six days later, he'd disappeared. His dead body, showing signs of torture, was found in the trunk of a car.

As a teen, Ronald had been coerced into serving as a lookout for MS-13. "If I refused, they [would] kill me or kill my family members," he testified on his asylum application. He expected that the gang's well-documented practice of killing noncollaborators would speak to his plight. Immigration officials instead branded him a "self-admitted MS-13 gang member."[22]

Ronald's case is hardly an isolated incident. Researchers at Columbia University have been tracking the deaths of migrants killed soon after being deported. So far, they've identified over sixty instances, with countless others still living in fear for their lives. The US government doesn't track these numbers.[23]

The administration has been unmoved by these deaths. In a 2017 statement, Attorney General Jeff Sessions declared: "Claims of fear to return have skyrocketed, and the percentage of claims that are genuinely meritorious are down." The presumption of guilt is branded onto migrants long before they've had their day in court.

22 Ibid.

23 Sarah Stillman, "When Deportation Is a Death Sentence," *The New Yorker*, January 8, 2018, https://www.newyorker.com/magazine/2018/01/15/when-deportation-is-a -death-sentence.

Many have written on the explosion of gang violence in El Salvador, but few do it as well as Juan Martínez d'Aubuisson, an anthropologist who has studied gang violence for over a decade. Following a devastating civil war, d'Aubuisson notes, "The country was in ruins. Its infrastructure was reduced to rubble, and its social fabric irremediably torn. El Salvador was a country of orphans, of the unemployed, the crippled and the lame."[24] It was into this power vacuum that the United States deported gang members en masse. The *maras* (gangs) that now dominate much of El Salvador didn't arise out of thin air—they were an American export.[25]

According to the Woodrow Wilson International Center for Scholars, an estimated 273,036 people have been displaced due to violence in El Salvador.[26] As many as 20,000 have died in the past three years at the hands of gangs. The number rivals the death rate of most countries at war.[27] While the majority of El Salvador's homicide victims are young men, women face the constant threat of sexual violence and coercion.

24 Juan Martínez d'Aubuisson, *See, Hear, and Shut Up* (New York: OR Books, 2019).

25 Ibid.

26 Jessica Tueller and Eric L. Olson, "The Hidden Problem of Forced Internal Displacement in Central America," Wilson Center, August 21, 2018.

27 Sofía Martínez, "Life under Gang Rule in El Salvador," International Crisis Group, November 26, 2018.

The police aren't much better. Salvadoran online magazine *Factum* has uncovered extrajudicial executions, sexual assaults, and widespread extortion from the force tasked with protecting El Salvador's vulnerable. Despite an extensive record of human rights violations, the Salvadoran police have been the recipients of tens of millions of dollars of US aid over the years. Often, the line between the police and the gangs is blurred: security forces often serve as informants for the gangs.[28] Those seeking to escape the unyielding violence won't find safety at the hands of police. El Salvador's poor are trapped between a rock and a hard place.

For nearly two decades, the US government has granted Salvadorans Temporary Protected Status (TPS). The program grants temporary legal status to certain migrants who flee armed conflict or natural disasters. But in January 2018, the Trump administration announced its plans to end TPS for Salvadorans. While, at least for now, the courts have blocked the administration's efforts on the basis of "animus against non-white immigrants," the status of TPS remains uncertain.[29] If the state gets its way, migrants previously protected by TPS will be subject to deportation. The case is likely to reach the

---

28 Mark Townsend, "Women Deported by Trump Face Deadly Welcome from Street Gangs in El Salvador," *Guardian*, January 13, 2018.

29 Catherine E. Shoichet, "Federal Judge Temporarily Blocks Trump Administration from Ending TPS," CNN, October 4, 2018.

Supreme Court, where a conservative majority is expected to side with the administration.

The move to end TPS in the face of El Salvador's extreme violence speaks to the profound dehumanization of black and brown immigrants. Pundits underplay their claims by declaring them economic migrants, as if poverty as a driver for migration were less valid than security concerns. In truth, you can't comprehend one without the other. Economic status influences who is preyed on by gangs and who is able to pay off their steep extortion fees.[30]

As they await their day in court, asylum seekers are forced to spend months or even years in detention centers. As the American Immigration Council asserts, "The US detains more protection-seeking families than any nation in the world."[31] Families are often detained in remote locations, far from access to pro bono legal counsel—and they're vastly less likely to be represented by counsel when compared to their nondetained counterparts. As

---

30 El Salvador's gangs demand steep extortion payments from civilians under threat of violence. Not only the rich face racketeering: in a nation where the minimum wage is some $200 per month, poor migrants report being forced to come up with $400 each month or face the gangs' reprisal. Extortion also makes up a central source of income for MS-13 and Calle 18, the two gangs that dominate El Salvador; experts claim these rackets pull in hundreds of millions of dollars per year. Anastasia Moloney, "Deadly Gang Extortion Rackets Drive Emigration from El Salvador," *Reuters*, May 16, 2016.

31 Ingrid Eagly, Steven Shafer, and Jana Whalley, "Detaining Families: A Study of Asylum Adjudication in Family Detention," *106 California Law Review* 785 (2018), https://ssrn.com/abstract=3175027.

in Ronald's case, prolonged, indefinite detention is often used to terrorize migrants into self-deporting.

A second deportee, Miguel Panameño, was found buried in the same graveyard.

THE FIRST DATE

A bottle of cologne. A dirt-stained stuffed animal. A rosary. These are a few of the objects seized from migrants as they are apprehended by US Border Patrol. Tom Kiefer, a former janitor for Customs and Border Protection, quietly set out to photograph the contraband, a testament to the lives of those caught in the machinery of the US immigration system.

"I would see a rosary, a Bible, a bunch of toothbrushes. I didn't know what I was going to do with these objects but they were obviously part of a bigger, much larger story," he tells Springboard Exchange.[32]

"These objects represent their hopes, their dreams, their desires. . . . The objects I found made it to the bitter end: they weren't discarded. That's why I feel it's important to present these in a beautiful, dignified way, and a way for the viewer to let them think about what this represents—the dehumanization, the struggle, the

---

32 Nicole Rupserburg, "Photographer Tom Kiefer Documents the Things That Are Carried across the Border," Springboard Exchange, March 16, 2017.

desire. Is this what we feel is important to strip from these people? These items they carried with them? I would find a bottle of cologne and think, why would they bring that with them? Because they're thinking about their first job interview, or maybe their first date. I'm going to photograph that bottle of cologne in a way that is respectful. It's not what you would typically think of seeing when talking about immigration and people crossing the desert. It might make people think, 'Oh my God, that's the cologne I use.'"

So far, CBP's practice of stripping migrants of their belongings continues, and no one is spared. Border Protection agents made headlines in the summer of 2018 for confiscating stuffed animals amid the family separation crisis; even this minor source of comfort is denied to "undesirable" immigrants.[33] Anything deemed nonessential and potentially lethal—language CBP takes to its broadest interpretation—is promptly seized, then often lost in limbo in CBP storage facilities. Often, migrants are deported without their possessions, leaving them stranded in unfamiliar territory without basic necessities like cash or identification.[34] In a system characterized by a lack of accountability at every turn, this move perhaps has the deadliest

---

33 Amamda Terkel, "Kids Taken from Their Parents at The Border Get Their Toys Confiscated Too," *Huffington Post*, June 20, 2018.

34 Walter Ewing and Guillermo Cantor, *Deported with No Possessions: The Mishandling of Migrants' Personal Belongings by CBP and ICE*, Special Report, American Immigration Council, December 21, 2016.

consequences: reports abound of deportees facing harassment at the hands of Mexican authorities due to a lack of ID. Without documentation or money, immigrants find themselves stranded, unable to afford food or shelter.[35]

CBP's gusto for putting migrants at risk extends beyond the self-serving: they've been found to dispose of even "valueless" personal belongings. One migrant testifies: "They made me throw away my notebook with all my phone numbers. They kept the rest of my stuff, but I needed that notebook to talk with my family; my stuff is not as important to me as my family is. I have my husband and three (U.S.) citizen daughters; the oldest is 12, I have one who is eight, and the youngest one is three. How do I let them know that I was sent back here?"[36] Others have lost engagement rings, cell phones, birth certificates, and more.

Kiefer left his job with CBP in 2014, but the dehumanization of migrants in their custody continues wholesale. An ACLU report published in May 2018 documents a pattern of abuse and violence enacted against migrants in detention.[37] Among the abuses are allegations that CBP officials "punched a child's head three

35 Ibid.

36 Ibid.

37 "ACLU Obtains Documents Showing Widespread Abuse of Child Immigrants in U. S. Custody," ACLU, May 22, 2018, https://www.aclu.org/news/aclu-obtains -documents-showing-widespread-abuse-child-immigrants-us-custody.

times, kicked a child in the ribs, [and] denied detained children permission to stand or move freely for days." Sexual violence, too, is rife—between May 2014 and July 2016, immigrants filed an average of one complaint per day alleging sexual abuse. (Previous reports were not adequately logged.)[38]

VIOLENCE AT THE COURTHOUSE

So, how does this system that leaves so many lives in limbo operate?

Politicians like to argue that immigrants should just "get in line" if they seek to live in the United States. This assertion betrays their ignorance—or perhaps just bad faith—about how our immigration system works.

There are a few primary ways to come to the United States "legally," and at every step the US immigration system sets hurdles for those seeking to obtain permanent status.

Asylum/Refugee Status

Each year, the United States sets a specific limit on how many refugees will be accepted into the United States. In 2017, the cap

---

38 Rebecca Merton and Christina Fialho to Thomas D. Homan, Claire Trickler-McNulty, John F. Kelly, John Roth, and Veronica Venture, April 11, 2017, Re: Sexual Abuse, Assault, and Harassment in U.S. Immigration Detention Facilities, http://www.endis-olation.org/wpcontent/uploads/2017/05/CIVIC_SexualAssault_Complaint.pdf

was set at 110,000 per year. Trump announced plans to impose a cap of 30,000 per year in 2019. In 2018, despite his stated cap of 45,000, the administration admitted only 20,918. Trump is not the first to come in under the target; though George W. Bush instituted a ceiling of 80,000, his administration only accepted 28,000.[39]

Those seeking refugee status face rigorous background checks and must prove, beyond doubt, that they have a "well-founded fear of persecution based on race, religion, membership in a particular social group, political opinion or national origin." Applicants are subjected to a "credible fear" interview, where they are forced to recount in excruciating detail the events that led them to flee. Migrants with valid claims to relief often find their cases tossed out because of minor inconsistencies in their stories, despite a wealth of scientific knowledge demonstrating that trauma impedes recall.[40] The interview process itself is often retraumatizing, triggering intrusive memories and flashbacks.[41] The bar to prove credible fear is only further complicated by the material realities

39 Julie Hirschfield Davis, "Trump to Cap Refugees Allowed into U. S. at 30,000, a Record Low," *New York Times*, September 27, 2018.

40 Mayra Gome, *Trauma-Informed Legal Advocacy (TILA) in Asylum and Immigration Proceedings: A Curated Selection of Resources for Attorneys and Legal Advocates*, National Center on Domestic Violence, Trauma and Mental Health, September 2016.

41 Katrin Schock, Rita Rosner, and Christine Knaevelsrud, "Impact of Asylum Interviews on the Mental Health of Traumatized Asylum Seekers," *European Journal of Psychotraumatology* 6 (2015), doi: 10.3402/ejpt.v6.26286.

refugees face: fleeing violence and persecution, they rarely have time to collect substantiating documents establishing persecution, such as hospital records or news clippings. Without these, claiming refugee status is inordinately difficult.

Asylum is a political protection offered to those who qualify for refugee status but are applying from within the United States or seeking admission at a port of entry.[42] They face the same harrowing application process, but the number of applications accepted is even lower. In fiscal year 2016, of 73,081 applications processed, only 20,500 individuals were granted asylum.[43] Though we might like to think of our justice system as impartial and objective, the approval process is ultimately arbitrary: your odds of success rely disproportionately on which judge is assigned to your case. Researchers at Syracuse University tracked asylum cases in the San Francisco Immigration Court over a period of six years. They found the odds of an application being denied varied from 9.4 percent to a staggering 97.1 percent depending on which judge oversaw a case.[44]

42 "Refugees and Asylees," Department of Homeland Security, April 1, 2019, https://www.dhs.gov/immigration-statistics/refugees-asylees.

43 Zuzana Cepla, "Fact Sheet: U.S. Asylum Process," National Immigration Forum, January 10, 2019.

44 "Asylum Outcome Continues to Depend on the Judge Assigned," TRAC Immigration, Syracuse University, November 20, 2017, https://trac.syr.edu/immigration/reports/490/.

Employment-Based Visas

Even those lucky enough to apply through an employer face an uphill battle: the employer must by law cover the application cost and legal fees—usually running many thousands of dollars—so selling an employer on the idea is rare. Further, the employer must make a bulletproof case that no American can effectively fill the job. If by some miracle you meet this exceptional standard, your status is still far from guaranteed: each year, the government receives some 200,000 applications for only 85,000 available visas.[45] Applicants thus are entered into a lottery system. If you hail from a country that sends a higher proportion of qualified immigrants to the United States, you face a longer wait due to per-country caps; at present, applications from India received in 2008 are only now receiving their green cards. [46] Once you obtain this status, you must wait a further five years before you become eligible to apply for citizenship. Those desperate enough to flee the scourges of poverty and indiscriminate violence have rarely had access to the sort of education needed to qualify for such an avenue to citizenship.

---

45 Lomi Kriel, "Explainer: Why Can't Immigrants Here Illegally Just Apply for Citizenship?," *Houston Chronicle*, January 29, 2018.

46 Ibid.

Family Reunification Visas

Under the family reunification process, green card holders and legal US residents are able to sponsor a family member. This is the most common form of authorized immigration to the United States: nearly 65 percent of all authorized permanent migration to the United States in the past decade has been through the family-based immigrant visa process. There are limits on the types of relatives that may apply based on the sponsor's specific legal status. The Trump administration seeks to severely limit family reunification visas, claiming these newcomers pose threats to US jobs and natural security.

For "unskilled" workers without family already in the United States, there is virtually no process, no "line," to apply for legal permanent status.[47] Only 50,000 green cards are offered to these workers annually, despite an applicant pool of over 14 million each year.[48] The United States is uncompromisingly clear about the sorts of immigrants it wants, and poor, "unskilled" workers are not among them.

Not only are these pathways to citizenship notoriously difficult and time consuming, but they're also fraught with danger. ICE

---

47 This term has been used repeatedly to downplay the contributions of lower-class work-ers, though these jobs require significant adaptability and talents.

48 "Can You Navigate the Immigration Maze to U.S. Citizenship?," news release, Reason Foundation, August 21, 2008; Sintia Radu, "The American Dream Roulette," *US News and World Report*, November 10, 2017.

has been known to conduct courthouse raids, detaining migrants in the midst of immigration proceedings. They're easy targets. Immigrants are not entitled to legal counsel in immigration cases, and navigating legal aid options while detained is nearly impossible; studies have found that only 14 percent of detainees have lawyers.[49]

The Immigrant Defense Project has been tracking ICE courthouse raids since 2013. They've found a consistent pattern of excessive and escalating force. Plainclothes officers stalk the premises and surreptitiously seize migrants once within view. One mother reported leaving the courthouse with her son when two plainclothes officers emerged and dragged the son into a car. Ignoring her pleas for help, another agent shoved her against a wall and demanded she "shut up"; "she did not know it was ICE agents who arrested him until she received a call from her son in an ICE processing facility later that day."[50]

The arrests are traumatizing not only to those within ICE's purview. Panicked reports of kidnappings are frequent, and no one is spared from gratuitous violence. ICE preys on survivors of domes-

---

49 Patrick G. Lee, "Immigrants in Detention Centers Have Meager Resources When Seeking Legal Help," *Pacific Standard*, May 17, 2017.

50 Immigrant Defense Project, *The Courthouse Trap: How ICE Operations Impacted New York's Courts in 2018*, January 2019, https://www.immigrantdefenseproject.org/wp-content/uploads/TheCourthouseTrap.pdf.

tic violence and human trafficking and minors facing neglect. In a separate instance, ICE agents physically assaulted an attorney who was eight months pregnant.[51] Collateral arrests are common, too, despite ICE's stated commitment to avoid them. In multiple instances, family members accompanying their loved ones to court have been summarily arrested.

Courthouse raids have increased in frequency by 1,700 percent under the Trump administration.[52]

ARE YOU AFRAID?

Ana Veronica ran for her life.

Fleeing an abusive husband, Ana Veronica journeyed through Guatemala and Mexico before reaching the United States. Upon entry, she was immediately detained by Border Patrol.

Ana's husband, she testified, had beaten and raped her. When she tried to leave, he threatened to kill her and her children. Ana quit her job in Santo Domingo and fled with her children to her hometown. A year later, her husband forcibly entered Ana's apartment, beat her, and threatened to kill her. Two months later he returned, forcing her into his car and raping her in an isolated

51 Ibid.
52 Ibid.

area. The threats didn't stop: Ana received letters warning that if she did not go back to him, she and her children would be killed.

Ana begged the police for help on multiple occasions. Her husband served a total of four days in jail.[53]

Ana Veronica submitted over four hundred pages of evidence—among them, a police complaint, a psychologist's assessment denoting her trauma, and a doctor's report substantiating physical assault and forced penetration.[54]

Her claim was found not credible.

In applying for asylum, much of an immigrant's fate hinges on whether they can demonstrate "credible fear." So just how is this fear—or lack thereof—assessed?

The interview is a bare-bones process. Applicants are at the mercy of whatever asylum officer is assigned to the case—their biases, preconceived notions, and all. For such a life-changing decision, there is little infrastructure in place to ensure a fair trial. Immigrants have no right to an immigration lawyer and can rarely access one from within detention. Hesitating to answer a question or stammering will elicit further questions. Minor inconsistencies can discredit an entire interview.

---

53 Ana Veronica Jimenez Ferreira v. Loretta Lynch, US Court of Appeals, Seventh Circuit, decided July 12, 2016.

54 Ibid.

Trauma is unyielding. Trauma does not *care* that one's life might hinge on the ability to regurgitate bits of information on demand. The symptoms manifest in a variety of ways. One person might be hyperaroused, always on edge, anticipating the next threat. Another may be numb and detached as a means to cope—but a judge might read the response as indifferent or untruthful. The sheer intensity of these memories can often render them difficult to convey narratively, more so when the migrant knows they will be punished for minor inconsistencies. Though the interviews are in theory meant to be nonadversarial, they are not recorded—an asylum officer's notes are the only record of the exchange.[55]

The risk of an incorrect assessment is great. Judges fundamentally rely on an applicant's presentation, candor, and consistency in gauging credibility. Applicants are effectively penalized for their trauma: as attorney Alana Mosley notes, "The focus is not actually on the facts of the case, but instead the applicant's unwavering consistency in relaying traumatic details."[56] The questioning process fails to address not only the cognitive impact of trauma but the enduring scars long after the fact. Is it so surprising that recent detainees, having faced police apathy and abuse back home, would be hes-

55 Alana Mosley, "Re-Victimization and the Asylum Process: Jimenez Ferreira v. Lynch: Re-Assessing the Weight Placed on Credible Fear Interviews in Determining Credibility," *Law and Inequality* 36, no. 2 (2018).

56 Ibid.

itant to trust authorities with their most intimate traumas? Given the stigma of sex and sexual violence, can migrants be expected to recount these experiences in perfect detail to a complete stranger?

In July 2016, the US Court of Appeals for the Second Circuit found that the immigration judge overlooked corroborating evidence in Ana Veronica's case. The process itself remains unchanged.

JAKELIN AND FELIPE

Jakelin Caal Maquin celebrated her seventh birthday on the migrant trail. Five days later, she was dead.

Jakelin's father set out with his daughter in hopes of earning money to send home. In their home village of Raxruhá, Guatemala, the family scraped by on $5 per day. Jakelin got her first pair of shoes in anticipation of the journey.

While Guatemala's industrialization has led to immense wealth for some, the country's poor are systematically excluded from this bounty.[57] Extractive industries like mining and hydroelectric plants have seen a significant rise in Indigenous territory, though the area's Maya inhabitants are rarely consulted. These projects have tracked closely with increases in the rape and murder of

---

57 According to census data, an estimated 54 percent of Guatemala's population lives in poverty. Guatemala's indigenous communities fare far worse—nearly 80 percent live in poverty, with half living in extreme poverty.

community leaders,[58] and have left Guatemala's poor to foot the bill from reduced health outcomes and environmental degradation and destruction. Meanwhile, promises of economic growth and job security fail time and again to pan out. An analysis of Marlin Mine, Guatemala's first large-scale gold mine, found that "the two nearby communities received only 5.1% of the revenue. Ninety percent of the revenue flowed to outside businesses, contractors, and, to a lesser extent, the national government."[59]

A Western consensus about the value of economic extractivism forced Jakelin to migrate. Weeks later, eight-year-old Felipe Gomez Alonzo followed her.

Hailing from the village of Yalambojoch, he too fled Guatemala's desperate poverty. Employment in the village is scarce, and life is precarious. The Guatemalan government has cast aside any obligation to indigenous territories, and malnutrition rates are among the highest in the world. For Felipe's family, the decision to migrate was painful yet inescapable; what parents could stand by and watch their children go hungry?

Felipe died on Christmas Eve.

58 Jeff Abbot, "In Guatemala, Indigenous Woman Sues Multinational Company for Husband's Murder," *TruthOut*, May 22, 2015.

59 Leah Shipton, "Canada's Mining Industry in Guatemala and the Right to Health of Indigenous Peoples," *Health and Human Rights Journal*, August 18, 2017, https://sites.sph.harvard.edu/hhrjournal/2017/08/canadas-mining-industry-in-guatemala-and-the-right-to-health-of-indigenous-peoples/.

INVENTING "ILLEGALS"

In her groundbreaking book, *Undocumented: How Immigration Became Illegal*, Aviva Chomsky speaks to the social construction of illegality. "The only thing that makes immigrants different from anybody else is the fact that they are denied the basic rights that the rest of us have," she asserts.[60] Anti-immigrant rhetoric maintains a veneer of neutrality by framing its opposition through respect for rule of law. But who is subject to a regime of surveillance and criminalization? As Dr. Chomsky asserts, "Becoming undocumented is a highly racialized crime."

Dr. Chomsky traces the evolution of the US immigration system from one that openly upheld racial quotas to one that merely enforced them in a more roundabout way. As Michelle Alexander writes, "In the era of colorblindness, it is no longer permissible to hate blacks, but we hate criminals."[61] Building on Alexander's seminal *The New Jim Crow*, Chomsky extends this logic of criminalization to immigrants. "Anti-immigrant . . . commentaries," she notes, "frequently

---

60 Aviva Chomsky, *Undocumented: How Immigration Became Illegal*, (Boston: Beacon, 2014).

61 Michelle Alexander, *The New Jim Crow: Mass Incarceration in the Age of Colorblindness* (New York: New Press, 2010).

emphasize the legalistic nature of their anti-immigrant sentiment: 'They broke the law!' But it's a law that, in design and in fact, is aimed at one, racially defined, sector of society."[62]

I spoke to Aviva about how this racialized system of control is maintained. "If you look at almost any society historically worldwide, there have been arbitrary decisions about who deserves rights and who doesn't. And those decisions, whether caste or enslavement, they define a certain group of people as inferior or undeserving."

Before long, Aviva notes, the distinction becomes naturalized and legitimated. Those who benefit from structural oppression feel justified in possessing rights that others lack: "From the outside, if you look back, you can see it's totally arbitrary. But in our own historical moment, we tend to be blind as to how it's happening in our own time and place, because it's been naturalized for us."

While our immigration system maintains a veneer of color-blindness, in truth the system is heavily stacked against nonwhite migrants. Dr. Chomsky points to a practice of *abstract liberalism*, perhaps best exemplified by Anatole France's famous words: "The law, in its majestic equality, forbids the rich as well as the poor to sleep under bridges, to beg in the streets, and to steal bread."[63]

62 Chomsky, *Undocumented.*

63 Andrew Sepielli, "The Law's 'Majestic Equality'", SpringerLink, November 27, 2012.

By treating everyone "equally," our immigration bureaucracy ignores historically constructed inequalities, whether social or economic. "We *supposedly* treat all countries equally in that every country has a quota. But countries are not all equal, neither in terms of population nor historically. Some countries are really big or tiny; if you grant an equal quota to a big and tiny country, that's treating the individuals in those two countries differently. European countries are not *explicitly* privileged, yet our laws do in fact tend to favor immigrants from Europe by treating every country equally," Chomsky continues.

Jeff Sessions's zero-tolerance policy of criminal prosecution for all unauthorized border crossings exacerbated these inequities. Immigrants are branded criminals, but it's an empty, circular logic: they're criminals *because we say they are*—because we have criminalized the very act of escaping violence. Obama's Felons, not Families policy illustrated that touting the deportation of "criminal immigrants" is an easier sell than copping to the deportation of parents or community figures, but this seemingly innocuous precedent allowed for the baseless criminalization of *all* migrants.

If we *really* wanted to explore criminality, the United States would not fare well. What other country has systematically undermined democracies across the globe with such vigor? What other country has wiped out entire families through drone strikes and military intervention in the "postwar era"?[64] Not only is criminalizing the basic act of human movement violent, but it sets America up for a conversation it would likely prefer to avoid. The United States has no moral standing to put criminality on trial: no nation is more steeped in violence and dispossession.

A LEGACY OF BLOOD

The America you know today was built on black and Native suffering.

Dating far back to colonial times, America's first immigrants came from northern Europe in search of economic opportunities and political freedoms. While proclaiming the virtues of freedom and equality, they cast aside these same principles where convenient, forcing African slaves to toil on stolen Native land. Indeed, European immigrants were responsible for the deaths of millions of African and Native people, a fact that is overlooked in flowery proclamations of "a nation of immigrants." These newcomers had no intention of ending the oppression they fled. They just wanted to be in the driver's seat.

Their descendants resented newer immigrants from southern Europe, and, as they settled, southern Europeans became suspect of the next influx of immigrants, and so on. Assimilation to

---

64 Ruth Sherlock, Lama Al-Arian, and Kamiran Sadoun, "'Entire Families Wiped Out': U. S. Airstrikes Killed Many Civilians in Syria," *NPR*, November 9, 2018.

whiteness was the metric by which immigrants were judged, and it was constantly shifting—through always informed by anti-blackness and a disregard for stolen Native land.

In the late 1630s, colonizers in New England clashed with the Pequot tribe over access to the fur trade. Colonist forces massacred tribal members leading to the near-eradication of the tribe. The few who survived were sold into slavery and prohibited from using the Pequot language under pain of death. Elsewhere in the colonies, Europeans received generous bounties for Native scalps—including those of children. Prior to colonization, an estimated ten million Native Americans lived in what is now the United States. By 1900, that number had dropped to three hundred thousand.[65] The 1830s saw the passage of the federal Indian Removal Act, which forced nearly one hundred thousand Natives off their land to fuel America's boundless hunger for expansion. Some four thousand Cherokee people succumbed to cold, hunger, or disease. California's gold rush only exacerbated the abuse of Native populations—in the twenty years following the discovery of gold, 80 percent of California's Native population was eradicated.[66]

In 1924, Native Americans were granted citizenship. On their own land. Even then, the struggle for Native rights was contested

---

65 Though disease played a significant role in the decline of Native populations, so too did violence, forced labor, and malnutrition at the hands of the colonists.

66 Erin Blakemore, "California's Little-Known Genocide," *History*, November 16, 2017.

every step of the way. The Indian Civil Rights Act—granting them nothing more than the protections already extended to other citizens under the Bill of Rights—would not come to be for another forty years. Strangers in their own land.

A convenient narrative persists that slavery benefited only a wealthy Southern minority. But the very roots of American wealth today can be traced back directly to slavery and racial terrorism across the nation. As Sven Beckert, author of *Slavery's Capitalism: A New History of American Economic Development, argues,* slavery was a national institution until the nineteenth century. Though its grasp was not as enduring, the North benefited indirectly even after moving away from direct enslavement of Africans: Northern merchants continued to sell slave-made goods and to rely on the economic powerhouse that was slave-grown cotton.[67] As Felice León, host and video producer at *The Root*, notes, "Over $600 million—or just about half of the country's economic activity in 1836—came directly or indirectly from cotton."[68]

The value of black landowners' losses alone is worth millions today. In the early 2000s, the Associated Press conducted an eighteen-month investigation and found a consistent pattern of

67 Sven Beckert and Seth Rockman, *Slavery's Capitalism: a New History of American Economic Development*, University of Pennsylvania Press, 2018.

68 Felice León, "Watch: We Built This," *Root*, September 16, 2017.

black Americans being driven from their land through violence, intimidation, or fraud. The investigation revealed over one hundred instances of dispossession, wherein landowners lost over twenty thousand acres of farmland. The vast majority of this property today is owned by white people or corporations.[69] Discriminatory housing policies exacerbated the black-white wealth divide: New Deal public housing projects were strictly segregated along racial lines, and government-backed lenders deliberately excluded black buyers. As a result, African Americans were limited to purchasing from private sellers who, encouraging white flight, bought homes at deep discounts and made steep profits off black buyers with nowhere else to go. Where economic pressure did not suffice, violence did: as Richard Rothstein notes, police tolerated and even directly supported cross burnings, arson, and other forms of violence to uphold residential segregation.[70]

Even renowned institutions of our time have slavery to thank for their status. In 1838, Georgetown University sold nearly three hundred slaves to finance the institution.[71] They pulled in the

---

69 Todd Lewan and Delores Barclay, "When They Steal Your Land, They Steal Your Future," *LA Times*, December 2, 2001.

70 Richard Rothstein, *The Color of Law: A Forgotten History of How Our Government Segregated America* (New York: Norton, 2017).

71 Profits from slavery have funded some of America's most prestigious schools, including Harvard, Yale, Columbia, and Princeton.

equivalent of $3.3 million in today's US currency.[72] Among the enslaved were pregnant women, children, and infants, some as young as two months old. A number of children were sold without their parents. When it comes to family separation, the United States has a short memory.

"WE DIDN'T CROSS THE BORDER, THE BORDER CROSSED US!"

Donald Trump is hardly the first to call for a whiter America. Though the language of enforcement may have changed, this racialized standard has underpinned US immigration policy throughout its history. What follows is a brief and greatly abridged survey of major US immigration policies beginning with the founding of our country.[73]

America's first immigration law, the Naturalization Act of 1790, limited citizenship to "free white persons" of "good moral character." Since then, the United States has attempted, with varying degrees of success, to restrict and exclude a changing cast of ostracized groups. As Ian Haney López, author of *White by Law*, asserts, "demographic change has historically led only to shifts in

---

72 Rachel L. Swarns, "272 Slaves Were Sold to Save Georgetown. What Does It Owe Their Descendants?," *New York Times*, April 16, 2016.

73 Volumes could be written about racism in US immigration law. See, for instance, David Scott FitzGerald and David Cook-Martín, *Culling the Masses: The Democratic Origins of Racist Immigration Policy in the Americas* (Cambridge, MA: Harvard University Press, 2014); and Chomsky, *Undocumented*.

where, not whether, racial lines are drawn."[74] Though the targets of racial resentment have altered with time, antagonism toward Blackness has been an ongoing theme.

The Alien and Sedition Acts, signed into law by President John Adams in 1798, extended the period necessary for immigrants to become citizens from five to fourteen years. They also allowed the president to deport or imprison noncitizens considered "dangerous to the peace and safety of the United States" or whose home countries were at war with the United States. While the first two provisions expired soon after the law was enacted, the last provision remains in effect today. The government made use of this during World War II to imprison "enemy aliens," many of whom were summarily deported after the war.[75]

The Indian Removal Act of 1830 did little to satiate US hunger for expansion. In 1845, the US government annexed Texas. In the spirit of Manifest Destiny, the United States invaded Mexico in 1846. At the war's conclusion, Mexico was forced to accept the US annexation of Texas and concede more than half of its remaining territory—including present-day New Mexico, California, Nevada, and Arizona. The land that was ceded was not unoccupied—its residents

74 Ian Haney-Lopez, *White by Law: The Legal Construction of Race* (New York: New York University Press, 2006).

75 Andrew Glass, "Congress Initiates Alien and Sedition Acts, June 18, 1798," *Politico*, June 18, 2018.

had long ties to the land. Though the original treaty stipulated that Mexican landowners would keep their property, the Senate removed this provision. Mexicans were forced to prove to US courts—in a language not their own—that they did indeed own the land. Predictably, Mexicans lost thousands of acres of land. For this reason, if you find yourself at a Chicano immigrant rights rally, you might hear the phrase: "We didn't cross the border, the border crossed us."

Following the emancipation of slavery in 1865, black Americans fought for the right to the land they had worked for generations. "Forty acres and a mule" became the rallying cry, in reference to Union general William Tecumseh Sherman's promise to enact agrarian reform. While the US government actively derailed Sherman's order, they concurrently granted millions of acres of cheap land to whites through the Homestead Act. While freed people were in theory able to apply, they had neither capital nor experience dealing with the government. More than 1.6 million white families received land under the Homestead Act. Only 5,500 African American petitioners did.[76]

The Chinese Exclusion Act, a federal law that prevented Chinese laborers from immigrating to the United States, was signed in 1882. The initial version of the act placed restrictions on certain Chinese laborers, but in 1924 the act was extended to citizens of other Asian

76 Keri Leigh Merritt, "Land and the Roots of African-American Poverty," *Aeon*, March 11, 2016.

nations and amended to ban Chinese nationals entirely. Though the Chinese Exclusion Act was the first to openly bar an entire ethnic group from immigrating, experts claim the Page Law of 1875 set the precedent for barring the immigration of "undesirable" immigrants; in that instance, women from "China, Japan, or any other Oriental country" were prohibited from entering the United States for "lewd and immoral purposes." Women seeking to migrate were subjected to a hostile line of questioning, including the following:

> Have you entered into contract or agreement with any person or persons whomsoever, for a term of service, within the United States for lewd and immoral purposes? Do you wish of your own free and voluntary will to go to the United States? Do you go to the United States for the purposes of prostitution? Are you married or single? What are you going to the United States for? What is to be your occupation there? Have you lived in a house of prostitution in Hong Kong, Macao, or China? Have you engaged in prostitution in either of the above places? Are you a virtuous woman? Do you intend to live a virtuous life in the United States? Do you know that you are at liberty now to go to the United States, or remain in your own country, and that you cannot be forced to go away from your home?[77]

77 George Peffer, *If They Don't Bring Their Women Here: Chinese Female Immigration before Exclusion* (Champaign: University of Illinois Press, 1999).

The Immigration Act of 1891 outlined new classes of undesirable immigrants, specifically those likely to become public charges, those convicted of crimes or misdemeanors, and polygamists. The act also prohibited advertising that encouraged immigration and allowed undocumented migrants to be deported. The act was challenged twice, and both times the courts ruled with the US government. The Immigration Act of 1903 expanded the earlier act's provisions with four additional excluded classes: anarchists, epileptics, beggars, and importers of prostitutes.

The Immigration Act of 1917 was the most ambitious immigration restriction of its time. The law established literacy tests for immigrants and further expanded the list of undesirables to include alcoholics, radicals, those with physical or mental disabilities, and the poor. The act also imposed significant restrictions on immigration from Asia by establishing an "Asiatic Barred Zone" from which people were prevented from immigrating.

Intensifying racial anxieties spurred the passage of the Quota Act of 1921, followed by a more restrictive version in 1924 known as the Johnson-Reed Act. The 1924 law set a total annual limit on immigration of 165,000. It also set quotas of 2 percent of any nationality, based on residency statistics from the 1890 census. This date was not pulled out of thin air; the baseline of 1890 was just before waves of migrants began to come from Southern and Eastern Europe. The consequences of this deliberate exclusion were made tragically clear when the

United States turned away Jewish refugees fleeing Hitler's war machine.[78]

The period between 1924 and 1965 saw immigration approvals to the United States slashed by 85 percent.[79] During the Great Depression, the United States expelled over a million Mexicans, more than half of them citizens.[80] Anti-Mexican resentment grew tremendously during this time, exacerbated by the advent of Operation Wetback (1954). The initiative led to a significant rise in arrests and deportations by US Border Patrol—an estimated 1.3 million people were deported or left their homes under threat of deportation in 1954.[81]

The Chinese Exclusion Act was repealed in 1943, thus allowing Chinese nationals in the country to become citizens. That this occurred sixty-one years after the act's initial passage—and only after China became an ally of the United States against Japan—speaks not to the waning of racism but rather to political expediency.

Explicit racial quotas were ended in 1965, although what followed was scarcely better. While the Hart-Celler Act abolished race-based

78 Rebecca Erbelding, "The Dark Political History of American Anti-Semitism," *The Hill*, August 21, 2017.

79 Natalie Molina, *How Race Is Made in America: Immigration, Citizenship, and the Historical Power of Racial Scripts* (Berkeley: University of California Press, 2014).

80 Francisco Balderrama, interviewed by Terry Gross, "America's Forgotten History of Mexican-American 'Repatriation,'" *Fresh Air*, NPR, September 10, 2015.

81 Ron Grossman, "Flashback: The 1954 Deportation of Mexican Migrants and the 'Wetback Airlift' in Chicago," *Chicago Tribune*, March 4, 2017.

quotas, these were merely supplanted by per-country limits that yielded the same effect. These ostensibly "colorblind" country caps didn't meaningfully differentiate between large and small countries; larger countries with significant migration to the United States such as Mexico and the Philippines had caps equal to those of smaller countries with infrequent migration. As a result, residents of larger countries with significant migration had to wait in line for citizenship nearly twice as long as some other foreign nationals.[82] Meanwhile, reform after reform continued to favor European immigrants. The 1986 Immigration Reform and Control Act—known mostly for criminalizing the hiring of undocumented immigrants—quietly increased the number of visas issued for several European countries.[83] The 1990 Diversity Visa program, too, sought to increase "desirable" immigrants by implementing a lottery for nationals of countries with lower migration. Of the nineteen countries declared ineligible for the program, all but three are in Latin America, the Caribbean, or Asia.[84]

The Immigration Reform and Control Act of 1986 established strict civil and criminal penalties for employers hiring undocumented immigrants. It also increased appropriations for the Immigration and Naturalization Service (INS), which at the time handled immigration

---

82 David Cook-Martín and David Scott FitzGerald, "How Legacies of Racism Persist in US Immigration Policy," *Scholars Strategy Network*, June 20, 2014.

83 Ibid.

84 Ibid.

enforcement, as well as the Executive Office for Immigration Review (EOIR), the agency that handled deportation cases. The law required the INS to increase the number of Border Patrol agents by 50 percent. As a minor concession, the bill offered a "clean slate" by granting amnesty to undocumented immigrants who met certain conditions, such as having resided in the United States since 1982. While this had a dramatic impact on the millions of undocumented immigrants who were able to obtain legal status, it came at a great cost. The law set the stage for dramatic expansions in Border Patrol capabilities.

From the late 1980s onward, the rate of immigrant criminalization skyrocketed. The 1988 Anti-Drug Abuse Act designated aggravated felonies as grounds for deportation. While this provision was initially limited to serious crimes such as murder and weapons trafficking, the subsequent 1990 Immigration Act eliminated discretionary relief and expanded the scope of aggravated felony. Four years later, the Violent Crime Control and Law Enforcement Act became law. The largest crime bill in US history, it added one hundred thousand new cops on the streets, expanded the death penalty, eliminated Pell Grants for incarcerees, and imposed a federal "three strikes" law that established a mandatory life sentence without parole for offenders convicted of certain crimes. Greater sanctions against "criminal" immigrants paired with the systemic overpolicing of communities of color have made for a deadly combination.

The Illegal Immigration Reform and Immigrant Responsibility Act (IIRIRA) of 1996 added further justifications for deportation and expanded the list of crimes constituting an aggravated felony. It further created expedited removal procedures and imposed more limits on judicial discretion. IIRIRA was an unprecedented attack on immigrants, paving the way for a regime of mass deportation.

The post-9/11 landscape exacerbated anti-immigrant hostility. The 2001 Patriot Act expanded the grounds for excluding immigrants from the United States and allowed for the indefinite detention of noncitizens.[85] The act significantly extended the definition of terrorism: a person could be charged for committing an act intended to "intimidate or coerce a civilian population; influence the policy of a government by intimidation or coercion; or affect the government by mass destruction, assassination, or kidnapping." This broad scope granted the government extensive powers to investigate and surveil the populace. Agencies have used the act to scare organizers and dissidents into silence. In July 2014, two animal activists were indicted and branded terrorists for releasing thousands of mink and foxes from fur farms. They were charged under the Animal Enterprise Terrorism Act (AETA), which was pushed through after heavy lobbying from the agri-business and fur industries and which exploited the Patriot Act's vague definition of terror activities.[86] This broad and undefined act

85 "How the Anti-Terrorism Bill Permits Indefinite Detention of Immigrants," ACLU, October 23, 2001.

86 "The Animal Enterprise Terrorism Act (AETA)," Center for Constitutional Rights, November 19, 2017.

has also been used to prosecute eight student activists for Palestinian solidarity organizing, despite former FBI Director William Webster's admission that none had engaged in terrorist activity.[87]

The Homeland Security Act, which created the department of the same name, became law in 2002. Thus, the INS was dismantled and replaced with US Customs and Border Protection (CBP), Immigration and Customs Enforcement (ICE), and USCIS, the agency responsible for overseeing naturalization processes. Under President Trump, the agency promptly scrubbed the phrase "a nation of immigrants" from its mission statement.

In 2006, Congress passed the Secure Fence Act, which mandated the construction of a fence along more than seven hundred miles of the Mexican border. In June 2012, the secretary of homeland security announced Deferred Action for Childhood Arrivals, known more commonly as DACA. The policy allows some individuals who were brought to the United States without authorization as children to receive temporary relief from deportation in renewable two-year periods. As of today, President Trump is attempting to dismantle the program.

The history of US immigration enforcement reveals a direct, sustained, and racist attack on immigrant rights. And yet, while

---

87 R. Jeffrey Smith, "Patriot Act Used in 16-Year-Old Deportation Case," *Washington Post*, September 23, 2003.

US immigration enforcement has always been racist, it is now bolstered by new advancements in technology—and the Trump administration's wholesale endorsement of ICE terror.

TERROR IN THE NIGHT

E. D. was nineteen years old when she was raped.

The young woman left her native Honduras fleeing sexual violence. Held in an immigrant detention center alongside her three-year-old son, E. D. was assaulted by a guard mere months into her stay. "I couldn't say no, I couldn't say anything," she says.[88] "I just did what he wanted."

Guards and administrators, "they all knew," says E. D.'s attorney.

Several thousand immigrants have reported sexual abuse within detention facilities. A 2013 Government Accountability Office report found that immigration detention centers failed to report 40 percent of sexual abuse violations.[89] Those that were acknowledged were written off: between 2012 and 2017, ICE found only 12 percent of complaints to be substantiated.[90] Those who come

---

88 Emily Kassie, "Sexual Assault inside ICE Detention: 2 Survivors Tell Their Stories," *New York Times*, July 17, 2018.

89 Victoria López and Sandra Park, "ICE Detention Center Says It's Not Responsible for Staff's Sexual Abuse of Detainees," ACLU, November 6, 2018.

90 Alice Peri, "Detained, Then Violated," *Intercept*, April 11, 2018.

forward about their abuse face retaliation—guards weaponize the threat of deportation to solicit compliance.

Only a landscape of fear and xenophobia could have produced the ICE we know today. At the time of the September 11 terror attacks, the agency's role was being filled by INS, an agency within the Department of Justice. But in the post-9/11 climate, fear of the "other" dominated. ICE was created and placed under what we now know as the Department of Homeland Security, a move that captured perfectly America's racial anxieties at the time. From its very inception, the agency viewed immigration through the lens of national security rather than, say, an administrative lens. Surveillance and suspicion of communities of color were built into the plan.

Secret detentions. Prisoner abuses. Unapologetic racial profiling.[91] The aftermath of 9/11 demonstrated just how much you can get away with in the name of safety. It's a lesson ICE has seized on. The agency delights in the terror of immigrant communities; in the words of former director Thomas Homan, immigrants "should be afraid."[92]

And they are. ICE raids are highly traumatic, and not only for those detained. Entire communities suffer. After a 2018 ICE raid at a Ten-

---

91 Irum Shiekh, *Detained without Cause: Muslims' Stories of Detention and Deportation in America after 9/11* (New York: Palgrave Mcmillan, 2011).

92 Tal Kopan, "ICE Director: Undocumented Immigrants 'Should Be Afraid,'" *CNN*, June 16, 2017.

nessee meatpacking plant, over five hundred students missed school the next day. When they did return, things were different. Students were unable to focus, trapped in a fog of fear and uncertainty. They weren't sure if anyone would be at home waiting for them. One child reported that every adult in his life was arrested during the raid.[93]

The practice has lifetime implications. Epidemiologist Nicole Novak tracked adverse birth outcomes before and after a 2008 immigration raid in Postville, Iowa—at the time, the largest immigration raid in US history. She found that infants born to Latina mothers had a 24 percent greater risk of low birth weight after the raid.[94] Over a decade later, the city is still on the mend. The raid claimed businesses and left a spate of foreclosed homes. "It was like they dropped a nuclear bomb on us," said one resident.[95]

Over the course of hours, Postville lost nearly one-fifth of its population.[96] Immigration officials stormed the town with assault rifles in hand. Workers were chased down the streets. People hid out in churches. Parents cried out for their children.

93 Ryan Devereaux and Alice Speri, "The Day after Trump's ICE Raid in a Small Tennessee Town, 550 Kids Stayed Home from School," *Intercept*, April 10, 2018.

94 Nicole L Novak, Arline T Geronimus, and Aresha M Martinez-Cardoso, "Change in Birth Outcomes among Infants Born to Latina Mothers after a Major Immigration Raid," *International Journal of Epidemiology* 46, no. 3 (2017).

95 Jessie Higgins, "ICE Raid Devastated Tiny Midwest Town; 10 Years Later, It's Still Recovering," *UPI*, August 29, 2018.

96 Ibid.

In the aftermath, children suffered the most. Losing a parent means economic hardship and instability. It means years of emotional trauma and paralyzing fear of separation. It means family fragmentation, housing instability, and interrupted schooling.

It means fear.

After immigration raids, community members are wary of public institutions. They're less likely to participate in schools, health clinics, and other social services. Trust in institutions breaks down.[97]

This fear has devastating consequences. Victims of domestic violence have stopped reporting their abusers.[98] Experience has shown them what is at stake. In February 2017, a woman seeking a protective order against her abuser was detained by immigration officials at the courthouse.[99] Who tipped them off? Only one

---

97 Society for Community Research and Action, Division 27 of the American Psychological Association, "Statement on the Effects of Deportation and Forced Separation on Immigrants, Their Families, and Communities," *American Journal of Community Psychology* 62 (2018): 3–12, doi: 10.1002/ajcp.12256

98 Hannah Rappleye, Stephanie Gosk, Brenda Breslauer, and John Carlos Frey, "Immigration Crackdown Makes Women Afraid to Testify against Abusers, Experts Warn," *NBC News*, September 22, 2018.

99 Katie Mettler, "'This Really Is Unprecedented': ICE Details Woman Seeking Domestic Abuse Protection at Texas Courthouse," *Washington Post*, February 16, 2017, https://www.washingtonpost.com/news/morning-mix/wp/2017/02/16/this-is-really-un-precedented-ice-detains-woman-seeking-domestic-abuse-protection-at-texas-court-house.

other person knew the time and place of the hearing: her alleged abuser.[100]

Under ICE's "sensitive locations" policy, agents are not to conduct raids at schools and places of worship unless they have extenuating circumstances. However, despite the chilling effect on public life, courthouses remain excluded from the policy.[101] In any case, this "policy" means little: in February 2017, a father of four was arrested by immigration officials while dropping his kids off at school. In a video of the arrest, the man's thirteen-year-old daughter can be seen sobbing with fear.[102]

Life in detention is terrifying and uncertain. Migrants apprehended at the border spend their first days in *hieleras*, or "iceboxes," Border Patrol facilities notorious for miserable conditions and bitterly cold temperatures. There, they face a dearth of medical care, squalid conditions, and the constant threat of violence.[103]

In May 2018, the ACLU Border Litigation Project published a groundbreaking report alleging systematic abuse in CBP facilities.

100   Marty Schladen, "ICE Detains Alleged Domestic Violence Victim," *USA Today*, February 15, 2017.

101   Scott Bixby, "ICE Courthouse Arrests up 1700% since Trump's Inauguration: Report," *Daily Beast*, January 28, 2019.

102   Anne Brangin, "A Father Whose Heartbreaking ICE Arrest Video Went Viral Could Be Deported Today," *Splinter News*, August 7, 2017.

103   Scott Neuman, "Migrants Allege They Were Subjected to Dirty Detention Facilities, Bad Food and Water," *NPR*, July 18, 2018.

ARMING ABUSERS

The report found that CBP officials use excessive force on children with shocking regularity. In one complaint, a young boy alleged that a Border Patrol agent "threw him down and smashed his head into the ground with his boot."[104] In a separate episode, a child was "run over by a CBP truck, which resulted in 'crushing damage' and 'significant trauma' to the child's leg." Multiple allegations assert that CBP officials use tasers on children without provocation, despite evidence that using the device on children can be fatal.[105]

Sexual abuse, too, is all too common. A sixteen-year-old girl in CBP custody reported that a Border Patrol agent threatened her in front of her child, saying: "Right now, we close the door, we rape you." In a separate instance, an agent "threatened a group of children with 'sexual abuse by an adult male detainee' and then brought an adult detainee to the juvenile hold room." One child who witnessed the sexual abuse of another female detainee was later inappropriately touched by the same agent.[106] ICE and CBP maintain a regime of silence through such retribution.

The terror of a raid can never be erased.

---

104 ACLU Border Litigation Project and the International Human Rights Clinic of the University of Chicago Law School, *Neglect and Abuse of Unaccompanied Immigrant Children by US Customs and Border Protection*, May 2018.

105 Ibid.

106 Ibid.

In April 2017, a group of agents armed to the teeth stormed through an apartment complex in Heber City, Utah. The agents burst into a home, screaming orders at Alicia and her grandchildren. They pointed their guns at the terrified grandmother and then at the children, none older than six.

They were looking for Alicia's husband, who had no criminal past but had been indicted for unlawful reentry years before. They brought assault rifles to detain a grandfather.

Realizing her husband was nowhere to be found, the agents detained Alicia. They "had to take somebody," an agent told her son.[107]

The nightmare was far from over. Over the course of the next day, an agent told Alicia's son they would be willing to "trade" her for her husband. When he didn't take the bait, the agent sent a single word.

"Congratulations."

That night, the agents broke through the apartment door with a battering ram. Asked to show a warrant, the agents laughed and called the family criminals. Despite having no record, Alicia now awaits deportation.

Families like Alicia's bear the scars of our immigration policy every single day. But some are fighting back.

---

107   McKenzie Romero, "Utah Family, ACLU Sue Federal Agents over 2 'Egregious' Raids," *Deseret News*, February 27, 2018.

ARMING ABUSERS

Inside an unassuming church in New York City, there is a flurry of movement. Families listen intently as a young organizer and a lawyer talk of *redadas*, or raids. Activists greet those seeking legal counsel—they call them Friends—with hugs. Children look on shyly before erupting into laughter. Life itself.

The New Sanctuary Coalition (NSC), an interfaith alliance opposing detention and deportation, has come together for its weekly immigration legal clinic during which volunteer attorneys walk migrants through paperwork for asylum claims and other issues. Though its volunteers hail from a wide variety of backgrounds, one thing is resolutely clear: the group stands in solidarity with all immigrants, whatever their circumstances.

NSC's accompaniment program pairs volunteers with immigrants en route to their court check-ins. It seems simple, but the stakes are high. Not only is the moral support crucial amid the uncertainty and possibility of arrest, but having an extra person in the room signals to the judge that people are watching and that the community will mobilize against deportation. In a system rife with abuses, it's a small way of holding officials accountable.

When not organizing clinics or accompaniments, NSC is expanding a community-based Sanctuary Hood program to organize safe spaces for immigrants. Through the program, local businesses and civic and religious institutions make a pledge to become sanctuaries. This can mean a lot of things, from providing a place to hide in the event of ICE raids to providing migrants with information and resources. They also run a bond fund to free migrants from for-profit detention centers. The organization moves quickly.

People have noticed. Membership of NSC has exploded in the past year. And as New Sanctuary has risen to national prominence, ICE has noticed too. In January 2018, ICE took custody of Ravi Ragbir, executive director of the NSC.[108] Ravi had entered the building willingly for a regularly scheduled check-in, the sort immigrants are subjected to as a routine matter. But such events are never really routine. At each check-in, the threat of deportation—and the suspension of all due process—looms. As word spread, faith leaders, friends, and activists supporting Ravi swarmed to block the vehicle's path, chanting Ravi's name for the better part of an hour while Ravi, handcuffed, yelled what could have been final goodbyes through the thin ambulance walls. Law enforcement used force to restrain the protesters, pushing Councilmember Jumaane D. Williams against the hood of a car and choking NSC cofounder Juan Carlos Ruiz without warning.[109]

It was the second arrest of a New Sanctuary leader within a week.

108 Carey Dunne, "Sanctuary Activists Say Trump Targeting Them after ICE Detains Second Immigrant Leader," *Village Voice*, January 12, 2018.

109 William Neuman and Liz Robbins, "Council Speaker Calls Police Response 'Out of Control,'" *New York Times*, January 11, 2018.

ICE has a long-standing—and intensifying—practice of silencing activists. Many have been detained shortly after speaking out against ICE, despite having no prior contact with the agency. In March 2017, a young activist was detained immediately after openly supporting DREAMers at a news conference. That same month, two immigrant-rights activists in Vermont were detained while campaigning for fair working conditions for immigrant farmworkers. In December of the same year, ICE began deportation proceedings against activist Maru Mora-Villalpando after she led protests against conditions in immigrant detention.[110]

E. D., the young woman mentioned at the start of this chapter, bravely filed suit against the detention center where she was held for the sexual abuse she experienced at the hands of staff. The center maintains that she consented.[111]

QUEER IN CUSTODY

Laura Monterrosa is a queer asylum seeker from El Salvador. Fleeing homophobic gang violence, she presented herself at the US border in 2017 and was promptly detained at the T. Don Hutto

---

110 Daniel Gonzalez, "ICE Arrests Aimed at Silencing Immigrant-Rights Activists, Critics Say," *AZ Central*, April 4, 2018.

111 López and Park, "ICE Detention Center Says It's Not Responsible."

detention center in Texas. A guard repeatedly groped Laura—at least two other guards witnessed this—before ultimately raping her.

ICE closed her case, finding that her account "could not be corroborated."[112]

Weeks later, she attempted suicide.

Navigating the complex bureaucracy of the US immigration system is rife with dangers. These are only exacerbated for queer and transgender immigrants. The statistics are dire: a 2018 report found that LGBTQ migrants are ninety-seven times more likely to be sexually abused in immigrant detention.[113]

While migrants are victimized for being visibly queer, so too are they penalized if they don't present in a way that reads "queer enough." The courts have long relied on gendered stereotypes to assess eligibility for LGBTQ asylum claims: in a 2007 ruling, an immigration judge asserted: "Neither [his] dress, nor his mannerisms, nor his style of speech give any indication that he is a homosexual."[114] Migrants early in transition or still exploring their gender

---

112 Mary Tuma, "Laura Monterrosa Released from T. Don Hutto," *Austin Chronicle*, March 23, 2018.

113 Julie Moreau, "LGBTQ Migrants 97 Times More Likely to Be Sexually Assaulted in Detention, Report Says," *NBC*, June 6, 2018.

114 Daniel Shahinaj v. Alberto R. Gonzales, US Court of Appeals, Eighth Circuit, decided April 2, 2007.

and sexuality throughout the asylum process have been found "not credible."[115]

S. A. C., a trans woman from Guatemala whose name has not been disclosed for privacy reasons, is no stranger to discrimination. Forced to turn to sex work after being fired for her gender, S. A. C. was raped by the Guatemalan police and threatened with death if she did not provide sexual favors for cartel members. The cartel threats were no empty words: one of her transgender friends had been killed at the hands of the cartel not long before. After hearing of LGBT protections in the United States, S. A. C. fled Guatemala in October 2016.

What she found was a far cry from those heralded protections. At the Stewart Detention Center in Lumpkin, Georgia, she requested that her preferred name be used. She was sent to solitary confinement shortly after.[116]

The National Center for Transgender Equality estimates that there are as many as fifty thousand undocumented transgender immigrants currently living in the United States. Those numbers

---

115 Stefan Vogler, "LGBTQ Caravan Migrants May Have to 'Prove' Their Gender or Sexual Identity at US Border," *Conversation*, November 30, 2018, http://theconversation .com/lgbtq-caravan-migrants-may-have-to-prove-their-gender-or-sexual-identity-at-us-border-107868.

116 Christine Bolaños, "For Trans Immigrants, the Road to Asylum Is Filled with Abuse and Frustration," *Remezcla*, December 4, 2017, https://remezcla.com/features /culture/road-to-asylum-for-transgender-immigrants/.

are likely underreported, as trans migrants can be hesitant to self-report for fear of violence. Undocumented trans immigrants often face challenges in accessing housing, health care, and basic social services. They also often find themselves shut out of jobs or education; when they can access these, they often face sexual harassment and unfair pay. Trans migrants face the deadly combination of rampant transphobia and hostility toward undocumented immigrants.

Once apprehended, trans detainees face significant challenges. They are housed according to the gender assigned at birth, which not only has significant mental-health implications but also increases their vulnerability to sexual or physical abuse. Often, detention facility officials will place trans individuals in solitary confinement to "protect" them. This means total isolation for up to twenty-three hours a day, despite well-documented concerns by psychologists about the effects of prolonged isolation. Even were it well intentioned, the practice does little to prevent abuse—if anything, isolation makes them an easier target for staff.[117] Trans detainees assert that their abuse often goes unreported because of the expectation that staff will not take their complaints seriously.

Trans detainees face invasive searches, routine harassment, and repeated denials of necessary medical care. They also face a culture

117   Ibid.

of impunity. In May 2018, Roxsana Hernández, a trans woman from Honduras, tragically died in ICE custody. While the cause of death appeared to be cardiac arrest, it later emerged that she had been beaten while in custody.[118] That she left her native Honduras fleeing violence—only to die within days of her arrival to the United States—speaks to the moral crisis that is US immigration enforcement.

After being detained for more than nine months at a men's facility, S. A. C. was finally granted asylum.

WHEN SURVIVAL IS A CRIME

I spoke to Geoff Kagan Trenchard, a lawyer and immigration activist from New York, about the consequences of how we—even the best intentioned of us—conceive of immigration.[119] For Trenchard, we won't get anywhere until we reassess the very way we approach the debate.

"Doctrinally, immigration law is an administrative concept; legally, it's governed under the administrative procedure act, like the IRS. But culturally, immigration is treated like a capital crime.

---

118 Emanuella Grinberg, "Transgender Immigrant Who Died in Ice Custody Was Beaten and Deprived of Medical Attention, Family Says," *CNN*, November 27, 2018.

119 Both Geoff and I are members of the NSC. Our views, however, do not necessarily reflect those of the organization.

"This was really codified after 9/11, when the immigrant/ terrorist analogy was hyped up to pass the Patriot Act, but you see the tenor throughout our whole history as a nation. The first immigration law in the United States specifically mentions the rights of white men. Immigration has always been tied to the maintenance of white supremacy the same way the prison system is."

As long as our immigration policy turns a blind eye to history, immigrants will be terrorized in the shadows. Decades of US intervention and pillage have spurred migration across the globe. What does the United States owe to those impacted by our violent legacy?

Well-meaning analysts like to argue that immigration benefits the US economy: *"They do the jobs we don't want to do!"* While this is certainly true, it ultimately misses the point. The moment we assess a person's worth by their economic contribution, we uphold the binary between the *deserving* and the *worthless*. Rather than seeking to expand who fits in the first category, it would be better to abolish this dichotomy altogether. Those impacted by US violence deserve not just our scraps, but a seat at the table.

"I think a lot about how if you were to walk into any bar and say 'I just came from bankruptcy court,' you would likely get a free drink from the bartender. There could be a Blue Lives Matter flag behind the bar, or a Black Lives Matter flag, and either way, you are getting at least a heavy pour," Trenchard continues.

"You could even tell the bartender, 'It was completely my fault. I worked off the books for a long time, I got divorced, I bought a boat for no reason,' and the bartender would still be sympathetic, no matter their political identification.

"So why does immigration elicit such a different reaction in the Blue Lives Matter bar? It's the same level of legal infraction. It's dealt with in an administrative court. But immigration is seen as an affront to an imagined racial/national identity. Specifically, American whiteness."

4

TOWARD FREEDOM

"¡La lucha obrera no tiene frontera!"
The workers' struggle has no borders!

When the news of Trump's family separation policy broke, the outrage was immediate. Photos of immigrant children in cramped cages prompted anger and criticism across the nation.

The only problem?

Those photos dated back to the Obama administration.[1]

Abolish ICE is more than a slogan. The agency's attacks on immigrant communities increase each day in scope and terror, whatever party is in charge. Unconstitutional searches. Sexual violence. Wanton abuse. ICE cruelty has shown us that no reforms or oversight will fix this. What is there to salvage in an agency that exists solely to hunt, detain, and terrorize immigrants?

Is a lofty goal, and that reform is the only means of change in our lifetime. But we must dare to dream bigger. Comprehensive immigration reform has meant minor concessions to some at a great cost for the many. It has meant upholding the binary of

---

1   Also, it was Customs and Border Protection who was behind the family separation policy, but we'll get into that. But still, fuck Trump.

"good" and "bad" immigrants, where *goodness* is always conditional and easily revoked. It means being held to a standard of scrutiny that no US citizen could bear. Immigration reform has won us filthy detention centers and agents that operate in the shadows. We can, and must, do better.

So, what does abolition mean?

It means asserting that no human being is illegal. That migration is not a crime, but as enduring as human history itself. That we will not collaborate with an immoral agency.

What would it look like if the border were staffed with social workers ready to engage with the complex process of trauma, instead of with heavily militarized agents predisposed to see migrants as an invading, hostile force?

What would it look like if the United States acknowledged its role in inciting violence and hunger across the globe for generations? If it committed to righting these historical wrongs by way of reparations and cancellation of foreign debt? If we were to cast aside detached assessments of *what is realistic* and instead stand strong in refusing to accept this state of affairs?

Abolishing ICE alone won't undo centuries of repressive immigration laws. It won't fix racialized "tough on crime" policies that aggressively criminalize communities of color. It won't do away with CBP, whose bloodlust for terrorizing those without a voice has gained them notoriety around the globe. The work cannot and must not stop at dismantling the agency. But it would be an important start.

It comes down to this: What sort of world do we want to live in? One where capital moves more freely than people, where immigrants are hunted and criminalized? Or one that recognizes human movement as not only an inevitability but a basic human right?

Abolishing an agency that hunts, assaults, and terrorizes human beings is not radical. Allowing it to continue is.

BY ANY MEANS NECESSARY

Activists have a vision for bringing an end to the agency. And, crucially, they have many successes to build on.

In 2016, the advocacy group Freedom for Immigrants filed a complaint against California's Santa Ana City Jail, detailing systematic violations of the human rights of detainees. Notorious for invasive strip searches and transphobic treatment of detainees, the facility faced mounting pressure from immigrant rights organizers and ultimately announced its decision to end its contract with ICE.[2]

The momentum is building. In June 2018, Williamson County voted to end its contract with ICE for the operation of the T. Don

---

2 Christina Fialho, *Rebuilding Trust: A Case Study for Closing and Repurposing Immigration Detention Facilities*, Freedom for Immigrants, February 2018.

Hutto detention center after a series of sexual assault allegations.[3] Just three months later, Atlanta mayor Keisha Lance Bottoms signed an executive order declaring that the city would no longer hold detainees for ICE. "Atlanta will no longer be complicit in a policy that intentionally inflicts misery on a vulnerable population without giving any thought to the horrific fallout," Bottoms declared.[4]

These successes show the value of sustained and localized pressure campaigns. And, as activists have demonstrated, individual localities need not be the only subjects of our scrutiny. One crucial strategy is targeting those who do business with ICE.

WHO PROFITS?

Zero tolerance is big business for US corporations. From private prisons to tech conglomerates, companies across the globe are scrambling for a piece of the pie. The Department of Homeland Security has awarded billions in federal contracts to surveil, detain, and terrorize immigrants.

Just a week after the 2016 election, stock prices for the nation's two largest prison companies rose by nearly a third. In June 2018

---

3   Calily Bien and Will DuPree, "Williamson County Terminates Contract with ICE, T. Don Hutto Facility," *KXAN*, June 26, 2018.

4   Jeremy Redmon, "Atlanta Calls for ICE to Move Its Detainees out of the City Jail," *Atlanta Journal-Constitution*, September 6, 2018.

they rose further on the assumption that they would benefit from the expansion of family detention facilities throughout the country amid the child separation crisis at the border.

Just what sort of company could bear to profit from the indefinite detention of children? Meet CoreCivic and GEO Group.

CoreCivic drew international scorn following the death of a toddler shortly after release from one of its detention facilities in May 2018. Mariee Newberry Juárez and her mother fled violence in Guatemala and were apprehended near the border. In immigrant detention, they were forced to sleep on the floor in a locked cage with some thirty other people. The young girl fell ill in the overcrowded detention center. Her fever spiked, and she began to vomit and suffer from diarrhea. A nurse cleared her for release without examining her. She succumbed to illness soon after and died just weeks before her second birthday.[5]

CoreCivic has a long and storied history of scandal. In 1999, the Colorado Department of Corrections investigated the company on allegations of brutality, sexual misconduct, and drug trafficking.[6] A 2011 audit of one of its facilities found violence, substandard

---

5   "Notice of Claim for Damages under the Federal Tort Claims Act—Yazmin Juárez (on Behalf of Herself and Her Deceased Daughter," Arnold & Porter Kaye Scholer LLP, November 27, 2018; the claim can be accessed at https://www.arnoldporter.com/en /perspectives/news/2018/11/ap-files-claim-against-ice-cbp-dhs-hhs.

6   "CCA Facility Cited for Sex Scandal," *Prison Legal News*, March 15, 2000, https://www .prisonlegalnews.org/news/2000/mar/15/cca-facility-cited-for-sex-scandal/.

medical treatment, and "unacceptable living conditions."[7] That same year, a second facility faced a class-action lawsuit due to allegations of sexual assault against migrant women in detention.[8] In 2017, the Department of Justice issued a scathing report on a separate facility alleging poor oversight and overcrowding.[9] In 2018, the corporation was sued for violating human trafficking laws.[10]

Not to be outdone, GEO Group has no shortage of scandals. In 2007, GEO settled a suit concerning a detainee who committed suicide following her rape within the facility.[11] In 2013, inmates at a GEO-run correctional facility sued the state, alleging "barbaric and horrific conditions." Incarcerees faced a desperate lack of medical and mental health treatment, lived in unsanitary conditions, and were subjected to excessive use of force.[12] In January

---

7 Chris Kirkham, "Lake Erie Correctional Institution, Ohio Private Prison, Faces Concerns about 'Unacceptable' Conditions," *Huffington Post*, February 2, 2013.

8 "ACLU of Texas Today Files Federal Lawsuit on Behalf of Women Assaulted at T. Don Hutto Detention Center," ACLU, press release, October 19, 2011.

9 Office of the Inspector General, US Department of Justice, *Audit of the United States Marshals Service Contract No. DJJODT7C0002 with CoreCivic, Inc., to Operate the Leavenworth Detention Center*, Audit Division 17-22, April 2017, https://oig.justice .gov/reports/2017/a1722.pdf.

10 Azadeh Shahshahani, "Why Are For-Profit US Prisons Subjecting Detainees to Forced Labor?," *Guardian*, May 17, 2018.

11 Brendan Fischer, "Violence, Abuse, and Death at For-Profit Prisons: A GEO Group Rap Sheet," *PR Watch*, September 26, 2013.

12 *DOCKERY V. HALL*, ACLU, Mar 2, 2017.

2018, GEO Group settled a sexual harassment lawsuit to the tune of $550,000.[13] In August of that same year, a federal judge certified a class-action lawsuit against GEO for wage theft.

How do these companies that just can't stay out of the spotlight continue to win contracts from the government year after year?

GEO Group and CoreCivic have given nearly $9 million to political candidates and state parties over the past decade and a half, with an additional $3 million spent each year on lobbying.[14] The two spent nearly half a million dollars on Trump's candidacy and inauguration alone.[15] Allegations of bribery and malfeasance abound. In November 2017, CoreCivic allegedly capitalized on Montana's budget crisis to secure a renewal of their multimillion-dollar contract. In exchange for an extended contract, the corporation offered to return $34 million the state had placed in a "buy back" fund.[16] That same year, the Mississippi state attorney general announced a suit against GEO Group for bribing Mississippi officials to secure lucrative contracts. Christopher Epps, former commissioner of the Mississippi

13 Marcia Heroux Pounds, "Boca-Based Prison Operator Geo Group to Pay $550,000 to Settle Sexual Harassment Lawsuit," *Sun Sentinel*, January 8, 2018.

14 Timothy Williams and Richard A. Oppel Jr., "Escapes, Riots and Beatings. But States Can't Seem to Ditch Private Prisons," *New York Times*, April 10, 2018.

15 Ibid.

16 S. K. Rossi, "Private Prison Giant CoreCivic Manipulates Montana into Renewing Its Contract," ACLU, August 8, 2018.

Department of Corrections, was sentenced to nearly twenty years for accepting almost $1.5 million in kickbacks from companies seeking state prison contracts. GEO Group denies any wrongdoing.[17]

CoreCivic and GEO Group have a designated occupancy guarantee, requiring states to pay steep charges if they fall below the required number of inmates. Some facilities are contractually guaranteed to be up to 96 percent full.[18] To house a single detainee in a for-profit adult facility, the United States pays $148 per day. Contrast that with the $4 per-day cost for nondetention programs, and you can see where the state's priorities lie.[19] In 2018, ICE spent more than $800 million in taxpayer money on private detention centers.[20] When mass incarceration is this lucrative, it's little wonder that immigration arrests are skyrocketing.[21]

It doesn't stop there. Arizona's notorious SB 1070—which legal experts, almost without exception, have lambasted as legalized

17 Jimmie E. Gates, "Chris Epps Sentenced to Almost 20 Years," *Clarion Ledger*, May 24, 2017.

18 "The Corrections Corporation of America, by the Numbers," *Mother Jones*, July/August 2016.

19 Madison Pauly, "Trump's Immigration Crackdown Is a Boom Time for Private Prisons," *Mother Jones*, June 2018.

20 Nicole Goodkind, "ICE Used Taxpayer Money to Pay Private Prisons $800 Million to Detain Migrants in 2018: Report," *Newsweek*, December 27, 2018.

21 Anna Giartelli, "ICE Arrests of Illegal Workers, Employers up 700 Percent in 2018," *Washington Examiner*, December 11, 2018.

racial profiling[22]—itself came into law by similar means. The law requires police officers to demand proof of immigration status in the face of "reasonable suspicion" when detained or arrested. An NPR investigation found that high-ranking officials from the Corrections Corporation of America attended the policy's drafting. Of the thirty-six senators who cosponsored the bill, thirty received donations from prison lobbyists or prison companies.[23] Jan Brewer, Arizona's governor at the time, also had links to the prison industry: both her spokesperson and campaign manager were former industry lobbyists. Four days after the bill hit her desk, it was signed into law.[24] A month later, GEO Group had a conference call with investors. They cited immigrant detention as a growth opportunity.[25] Hunting immigrants became a viable business model.

Tech companies, too, are seeing a significant windfall. Amazon made national news in October 2018 for pitching its facial recognition software to ICE. The proposal would allow ICE to track migrants in real time, vastly expanding ICE's policing capabilities

---

22 Paige Newman, "Arizona's Anti-Immigration Law and the Pervasiveness of Racial Profiling," *Georgetown Law* 31, no. 3 (Spring 2017).

23 Laura Sullivan, "Prison Economics Help Drive Ariz. Immigration Law," *NPR*, October 28, 2010.

24 Ibid.

25 Ibid.

and signaling an end to refuge for migrants.[26] As it stands, ICE has targeted immigrants trying to access medical care and homeless shelters.[27] Armed with this technology, ICE could expand its surveillance powers tenfold, shadowing communities of color in perpetuity. This technology is so readily abused that even former ICE officers have expressed their concerns.[28]

The complicity goes further. HP, Thomson Reuters, Microsoft, Motorola, and Palantir all have active contracts with DHS.[29] ICE maintains a massive database to track and surveil immigrant populations. So vast is this infrastructure that IT spending makes up nearly 10 percent of DHS's budget—the largest IT budget across the government.[30] This extreme level of surveillance sets a precedent that opens the door to expanding mass surveillance further.

Though ICE is well entrenched, there are successes on which we can model our tactics. In June 2018, Google vowed not to extend

26 Russel Brandom, "Amazon Is Selling Police Departments a Real-Time Facial Recognition System," *Verge*, May 22, 2018.

27 Wynne Davis, "ICE Detains Man Driving His Wife to Hospital for Planned C-Section," *NPR*, August 19, 2018; Alex Emmons, "Targeting a Sanctuary: After ICE Stakes out a Church Homeless Shelter, Charities Worry Immigrants Will Fear Getting Help," *Intercept*, February 27, 2017.

28 Jake Laperruque and Andrea Peterson, "Amazon Pushes ICE to Buy Its Face Recognition Surveillance Tech," *Daily Beast*, October 23, 2018.

29 Erin Corbett, "Tech Companies Are Profiting off ICE Deportations, Report Shows," *Fortune*, October 23, 2018.

30 Ibid.

its contract with the Department of Defense after a sustained employee backlash. Thousands of Google employees wrote an open letter condemning the company's involvement in developing drone combat technology, citing Google's former motto: "Don't be evil."[31]

Building on this victory, workers circulated open letters at Microsoft and Amazon calling on chief executives to end their immigration contracts. Meanwhile, immigrant-rights organizers Movimiento Cosecha launched their #NoBusinessWithICE campaign, urging supporters to boycott companies and institutions cooperating with ICE. As Cosecha organizers declare, anyone profiting from the agency is complicit in family separation and ICE abuses.

It is not only those who have direct contracts with ICE that reap the benefits. US businesses hiring undocumented workers offer dismal working conditions and wages far under the legal minimum, knowing workers are unlikely to complain for fear of drawing attention. Workers who do speak up pay the price. Businesses have been known to call ICE on employees who demand better conditions or suffer workplace injuries.[32] Employers are using ICE as their personal enforcers.

31 Hallie Detrick, "Google Passes on a $10 Billion Pentagon Cloud Contract, Citing Its New AI Principles," *Fortune*, October 9, 2018.

32 Paul Harris, "Undocumented Workers' Grim Reality: Speak Out on Abuse and Risk Deportation," *Guardian*, March 28, 2013.

So strong is the fear of workplace raids that the Department of Labor reports being unable to conduct workplace investigations. As one workplace inspector reported, "They're not just refusing to talk to us. They're running away from us."[33] Another Department of Labor employee reports undocumented workers refusing back wages owed to them in order to avoid any contact with the federal government. Employers benefit significantly from this climate of fear.

Critics say undocumented workers create downward pressure on wages across the board. But while immigrants are scapegoated, it's businesses who won't pay up. Curiously, those who argue that immigrants drive wages down often claim in the same breath that competition benefits everyone. More feasible than putting an end to human migration would be simply writing the problem out of existence. Amnesty would fix any downward pressure on wages by neatly eliminating this wage differential. If employers can't exploit the vulnerable position of desperate workers, workers lose no bargaining power to new arrivals.

Academia, too, is implicated. Colleges and universities across the nation have contracts with ICE for a whole host of services. Northeastern University faced protests as the news of its $7,750,000 research contract came to light. Johns Hopkins, meanwhile, pulled

---

33 Sam Levin, "Immigration Crackdown Enables Worker Exploitation, Labor Department Staff Say," *Guardian*, March 30, 2017.

in $6.5 million for leadership and tactical trainings. Students at both institutions have urged their schools to cut their contracts. They must keep the pressure up. Even terminating smaller, more mundane contracts—like leased parking spots—can disrupt ICE's operations when such efforts are coordinated.

CRIMINALIZING DISSENT

No More Deaths, the humanitarian aid group conducting water drops across the Sonoran Desert, has attracted the wrong sort of attention. In January 2019, four volunteers were convicted for leaving water and food for migrants in the desert. The judge, Magistrate Bernardo P. Velasco, ruled that the defendants willfully broke the law by entering the Cabeza Prieta National Wildlife Refuge without a permit.

"The Defendants did not get an access permit, they did not remain on the designated roads, and they left water, food, and crates in the Refuge," Velasco wrote. "All of this, in addition to violating the law, erodes the national decision to maintain the Refuge in its pristine nature."[34]

The news of the rulings came as the *Intercept* uncovered hundreds of pages of government correspondence detailing the

34 Nicole Ludden, "What's Next for No More Deaths after Latest Convictions of Volunteers?," *Tucson Sentinel*, January 30, 2019.

close monitoring of No More Deaths volunteers; federal wildlife officers were instructed to deny permits to any suspected members of the group and disposed of humanitarian relief supplies found on their patrols.[35]

The US government has attempted, with unyielding insistence, to brand humanitarian relief workers as criminals. Scott Warren, the aid worker mentioned earlier who now faces up to twenty years in prison, was indicted on human smuggling charges. Judge Velasco, in announcing his ruling, appealed to the need to protect nature.

Do not be swayed by language of law and order. For this is what the law allows: Border Patrol officers, armed for war, can stalk migrants through unfamiliar terrain. Toddlers and their desperate mothers can die a slow and painful death in the desert. But those who seek to provide relief in this hopeless terrain face the full wrath of the law under the guise of environmental protection. Distributing water is a crime because it disturbs nature—as if there is anything natural about the human remains littering the desert.

No More Deaths volunteers are facing charges for providing lifesaving food and water to the most vulnerable among us. Humanitarian aid is not a crime.

---

35 Ryan Devereaux, "As Trial Starts for Border Humanitarian Volunteers, New Documents Reveal Federal Bureaucrats' Obsession with Stopping Activists," *Intercept*, January 17, 2019.

WHAT IS ABOLITION?

One of the dangers of the demand to abolish ICE is that it risks being watered down and used for electoral gain. We must not moderate our demands or succumb to respectability politics but instead demand basic human dignity for all immigrants. We call for abolition, for full and unconditional amnesty, not to see ICE's functions replaced in a Democratic establishment with better branding.

Abolition Means Defunding

ICE spends billions of dollars each year—$7.5 billion in fiscal year 2018—to harass and terrorize our communities.[36]

With $7.5 billion dollars, the United States could do any of the following:

- Fix Flint's pipes 136 times[37]
- More than double the budget of the Substance Abuse and Mental Health Services Administration[38]

---

36 "Fact Sheet: Immigration and Customs Enforcement (ICE)," National Immigration Forum, July 10, 2018, https://immigrationforum.org/article/fact-sheet-immigration -and-customs-enforcement-ice/.

37 Oliver Millman, "Elon Musk Pledges to Fix Flint's Water Contamination Crisis," *Guardian*, July 12, 2018.

38 Department of Health and Human Services FY 2018, Substance Abuse and Mental Health Services Administration, Justification of Estimates for Appropriations Committees

- More than double funding to combat the opioid epidemic[39]
- Fund the National Endowment for the Arts for another forty-nine years[40]

In September 2018, the news broke that ICE was lobbying for an additional $1 billion to meet its deportation targets.[41] This request came weeks after the Department of Homeland Security rerouted $10 million from the Federal Emergency Management Agency (FEMA) to ICE just as Hurricane Florence barreled toward the East Coast. Activists moved quickly. The #DefundHate coalition, comprised of grassroots and immigrant-led advocacy groups, launched a sweeping campaign. Coalition members met with thirty members of Congress in Washington, DC, and mobilized organizers to put pressure on their elected officials across the country. After countless petitions, phone calls, and protests, the Senate released a bill without ICE's requested funding.[42]

---

39 German Lopez, "Congress's Budget Deal Doesn't Do Enough to Fight the Opioid Crisis," *Vox*, February 9, 2018.

40 Ted Johnson, "Arts Funding Gets a Boost in Omnibus Spending Bill," *Variety*, March 23, 2018.

41 Maria Sacchetti, "ICE Says It Needs a $1 Billion Funding Boost to Meet Trump's Aggressive Deportation Goals," *Washington Post*, September 13, 2018.

42 Kathryn Johnson, "We Stopped ICE from Getting an Extra Billion; Now Let's Defund It Totally," *Truthout*, October 15, 2018.

ABOLISH ICE

Undeterred, ICE requested an additional $2.8 billion for 2019.[43]

#DefundHate's victory shows what is possible when communities organize. The coalition continues to put pressure on Congress to defund ICE and CBP. In the face of systematic human rights abuses on the part of both agencies, the pressure is escalating.

It doesn't stop at home. Through the Mérida Initiative, the United States funds Mexican border enforcement to contain Central American migrants through raids and deportations. The United States has effectively exported outrage to its southern neighbor, letting Mexico take the blame for apprehending migrants seeking to reach the United States. Apprehension of Central American migrants at Mexico's southern border has exploded. Much like Operation Gatekeeper, this program has done little to stem the flow of migration, only rerouting it to more dangerous terrain.[44] Congress must put an end to funding that puts people in harm's way.

Abolition Means Solidarity

Immigration is framed as a "Latino" issue with startling frequency. This reductive framing ignores the powerful diversity of

43 Bryan Lowry, "Arts Funding Gets a Boost in Omnibus Spending Bill," *McClatchy DC*, September 24, 2018.

44 Luis Alfredo Arriola Vega, *Policy Adrift: Mexico's Southern Border Program*, Mexico Center, Rice University's Baker Institute for Public Policy, June 2017.

the movement and the specific challenges that certain immigrants face. Black people are more likely to be stopped by the police, subjected to detention, charged with more serious crimes, and sentenced more stringently than their white counterparts.[45] Racial bias is systemic and touches every aspect of the justice system. Thus, black immigrants are disproportionately detained: "Although only 7 percent of non-citizens in the U.S. are black, they make up 20 percent of those facing deportation on criminal grounds."[46] Illegality is not an objective truth; it is through the intersection of our criminal justice system and our immigration system that that Black immigrants not effectively "made" illegal.

Abolition means centering Black people in our movements. It means calling for an end to predatory policing and standing in solidarity with communities most affected by police violence. It means not just demanding that police departments stop sharing information with ICE, but putting policing *itself* on trial.

It means acknowledging that black immigrants not only must navigate the violence of anti-immigrant vitriol but must bear the added weight of anti-blackness. It means confronting anti-blackness

45 "Research Confirms that Entrenched Racism Manifests in Disparate Treatment of Black Americans in Criminal Justice System," Vera Institute of Justice, press release, May 3, 2018.

46 Jeremy Raff, "The 'Double Punishment' for Black Undocumented Immigrants," *Atlantic*, December 30, 2017.

within and beyond our movements. It means confronting a system that puts our queer, trans, and gender-oppressed black comrades at special risk for state violence and economic exploitation.[47]

Abolition Means Reclaiming

Any immigration policy that does not acknowledge decades of US violence abroad is fundamentally incomplete. No longer will we allow the purveyors of violence to set the terms of the debate.

The moment we allow immigration to be framed as a matter of national security, we've lost. It's time to stop pretending the DHS—which ignores white nationalist terrorism as a matter of course—is acting in good faith in labeling migrants a security threat.[48]

Fear is motivating. It's easy to put a bloodthirsty monster into a cage. It's a lot harder to cage a family seeking refuge. By accepting a national-security frame for immigration, we concede that immigrants present a threat to our safety. Not only is this view dangerous, it flies in the face of US history. If anyone has been an aggressor on the global stage, it has been America.

---

47 Andrea J. Ritchie and Monique W. Morris, *Centering Black Women, Girls, Gender Nonconforming People and Fem(me)s in Campaigns for Expanded Sanctuary and Freedom Cities*, National Black Women's Justice Institute and Ms. Foundation, policy brief, September 2017.

48 Spencer Ackerman and Betsy Woodruff, "'Homeland Security' Ignores White Terror, DHS Veterans Say," Daily Beast, October 31, 2018.

Abolition Means Change

Abolition means an end to regressive laws that criminalize human movement. Much of the suffering in our immigration system today can be directly traced back to a pair of laws signed by President Bill Clinton in 1996: the Illegal Immigration Reform and Immigrant Responsibility Act (IIRIRA) and the Antiterrorism and Effective Death Penalty Act (AEDPA). These laws dramatically expanded the immigration-industrial complex by mandating detention of immigrants (largely in for-profit prisons), retroactively reclassifying low-level, nonviolent offenses as felonies, and eliminating defenses against deportation. As a result of the 1996 legislation, immigrants are criminalized and set up to fail.

Operation Streamline, too, penalizes migrants for the mere act of seeking relief.[49] Previously, immigrants apprehended at the border were passed through the civil immigration system. Now, the mere act of entry has been criminalized. Deported immigrants who reenter, seeking to reunite with their family, now face felony charges and up to two years in federal prison. Operation Streamline's zero-tolerance approach to border crossing was the backbone behind family separation. The program's impact can hardly be

---

49 A joint initiative by the DHS and Department of Justice that implemented a zero-tolerance approach to unauthorized border crossing by seeking criminal prosecution of those apprehended.

overstated: more than half of federal criminal prosecutions stem from these infractions, costing taxpayers $7 billion between 2005 and 2015.[50] Streamline's circular logic means that migrants are guilty by virtue of being migrants.

Abolition calls for a complete transformation of our immigration system. It means reimagining how we approach the question of immigration itself. Abolition means coming to terms with the inherent violence of borders. It means reparations to victims of US violence. It means life itself.

50 Bob Libal and Judy Greene, "It's Time to Decriminalize Immigration," *Texas Observer*, June 20, 2018.

EPILOGUE: SANCTUARY

A week before Christmas, Reverend Micah Bucey made his way to Tijuana from his New York City parish. The New Sanctuary Coalition had mobilized members across the country to provide legal aid and material support to the migrant caravan, a movement of immigrants fleeing gang violence and poverty, that was convening at the US border. The days were long, and desperation was palpable.

When faith leaders were available, the group would conduct weddings. They arose out of necessity—unmarried migrants in long-term relationships were being processed and sent to separate facilities. Marriage provided at least slim protection against being torn from one's loved ones. When couples would come into the legal clinic to fill out paperwork, they were concurrently offered the opportunity to formalize their union.

The first day, just a handful of couples signed up. It was a humble ceremony: the priest officiating at the services before Micah arrived had put together a packet with a basic liturgy, and the ceremonies were conducted on an empty rooftop.

The next day, someone brought a bag of rings that couples could choose from. After that, someone brought hand-picked flowers, then bouquets, and even *papel picado.*[1] Finally, a tray of Ferrero Rocher chocolates was procured, and thus were the newlyweds feted at their reception. Piece by piece, what was once a formality became a display of love and community.

Micah added vows from his own wedding.

With this ring, I give my promise that from this day forward, you will not walk alone.
My heart will be your shelter and my love will sustain you. When I am lost, I will look for you.
When you are lost, I will find you.
From this day forward, we will walk together, always.

1   A Mexican handicraft made by cutting elaborate patterns into tissue paper.

Want to get involved in the fight for immigrant justice? Here are some organizations doing powerful, immigrant-led activism. Please donate or get involved!

New Sanctuary Coalition (New York)
info@newsanctuarynyc.org

RAICES (Texas)
volunteer@raicestexas.org

No More Deaths (Arizona)
info@nomoredeaths.org

Familia: Trans Queer Liberation Movement (California)
info@familiatqlm.org